How Women Are Transforming Leadership

Recent Titles in Contemporary Psychology

Collateral Damage: The Psychological Consequences of America's War on Terrorism
Paul R. Kimmel and Chris E. Stout, editors

Terror in the Promised Land: Inside the Anguish of the Israeli-Palestinian Conflict
Judy Kuriansky, editor

Trauma Psychology: Issues in Violence, Disaster, Health, and Illness
Elizabeth Carll, editor

Beyond Bullets and Bombs: Grassroots Peace Building between Israelis
and Palestinians
Judy Kuriansky, editor

Who Benefits from Global Violence and War: Uncovering a Destructive System
Marc Pilisuk with Jennifer Rountree

Right Brain/Left Brain Leadership: Shifting Style for Maximum Impact
Mary Lou Décosterd

Creating Young Martyrs: Conditions That Make Dying in a Terrorist Attack Seem
Like a Good Idea
Alice LoCicero and Samuel J. Sinclair

Emotion and Conflict: How Human Rights Can Dignify Emotion and Help Us Wage
Good Conflict
Evelin Lindner

Emotional Exorcism: Expelling the Psychological Demons That Make Us Relapse
Holly A. Hunt, Ph.D.

Gender, Humiliation, and Global Security: Dignifying Relationships from Love, Sex,
and Parenthood to World Affairs
Evelin Lindner

Peace Movements Worldwide
Marc Pilisuk and Michael N. Nagler, editors

HOW WOMEN ARE TRANSFORMING LEADERSHIP

Four Key Traits Powering Success

Mary Lou Décosterd
Foreword by Carla L. Picardi

CONTEMPORARY PSYCHOLOGY
Chris E. Stout, Series Editor

AN IMPRINT OF ABC-CLIO, LLC
Santa Barbara, California • Denver, Colorado • Oxford, England

Library of Congress Cataloging-in-Publication Data

Décosterd, Mary Lou.
  How women are transforming leadership : four key traits powering success / Mary Lou Décosterd ; foreword by Carla L. Picardi.
    pages cm. — (Contemporary psychology)
  Includes bibliographical references and index.
    ISBN 978-1-4408-0416-8 (hard copy : alk. paper) — ISBN 978-1-4408-0417-5 (ebook) 1. Leadership. 2. Leadership in women. 3. Success. I. Title.
BF637.L4D427   2013
158'.4082—dc23   2013000772

ISBN: 978-1-4408-0416-8
EISBN: 978-1-4408-0417-5

17 16 15 14 13   1 2 3 4 5

This book is also available on the World Wide Web as an eBook.
Visit www.abc-clio.com for details.

Praeger
An Imprint of ABC-CLIO, LLC

ABC-CLIO, LLC
130 Cremona Drive, P.O. Box 1911
Santa Barbara, California 93116-1911

This book is printed on acid-free paper ∞

Manufactured in the United States of America

To my mother Rosemarie, our family's Dear Abby, Martha Stewart, and Billy Jean King all rolled into one. Mom, your color, love, and resolve are constant sources of inspiration.

To my Aunt Laura, whose kind praise and positive attitude have always been a treasured source of encouragement and validation.

To my Aunt Toni, whose giving nature and spot-on advice is an *anchor* for all of us, no matter what the struggle.

And to Nanny Lucy, our family's matriarch and feminist spirit—I miss you deeply (still) and work every day to be more like you.

Contents

Foreword by Carla L. Picardi   ix

Acknowledgments   xiii

CHAPTER 1   An Evolution of Influence: Women, Leadership,
             and Life   1
CHAPTER 2   An Intuitive Orientation   27
CHAPTER 3   A Woman's Directive Force   47
CHAPTER 4   Empowering Intent   73
CHAPTER 5   Assimilative Nature   97
CHAPTER 6   Where We Go from Here   117

Notes   139

Bibliography   147

Index   153

About the Foreword Author   159

About the Author and the Lead Life Institute   161

About the Series Editor and Advisory Board   163

About the Series   167

FOREWORD

How Women Are Transforming Leadership: Four Key Traits Powering Success by Mary Lou Décosterd, PhD, is a gift to all women interested in understanding their role as leaders and in transforming the people and the organizations they lead. Women are exercising leadership every day on numerous levels—often without realizing it—in our work, in our communities, and in our families. Because leadership is an activity, our subtle yet deep learning comes from who we are *being* as we lead. So it is wise and visionary for Dr. Décosterd to explore fully the question of *who* we need to be when we lead others and to describe clearly the fundamental characteristics that represent this feminine leadership model.

For too long we have confused the term "leadership" with authoritative power, and along with it have accepted the idea that *masculine traits demonstrate power* and *feminine traits reveal weakness*. Women entering the ranks of senior management have been guided by this one-size-fits-all masculine paradigm of power. In fact, we even thought that if we wore suits and acted like men we would be perceived as more powerful. In the early 1980s, I was an assistant vice president at Citibank, striving to be a vice president. I recall vividly my boss saying to me, "If you want that corner office, you need to look and act like you deserve it!" Over a decade later, after living outside of the United States for several years, I returned to find too many women who took that statement literally and became little men, with masculine mannerisms, clothing, and verbal presentation skills. I jokingly referred to it as the "asexualization of the American female executive"!

We did not need our male colleagues and bosses to set the height of our glass ceilings; we had already set the level of our own inner glass ceiling by not believing that what we had to offer had great value. We did not recognize that our feminine power, intuition, and wisdom had much more relevance to the success of our organizations than emulating the masculine version of power. We let this masculine model of leadership stand, and we squeezed into it like the good girls we were taught to be. We put our inherent nature aside because we did not realize as women that our way to lead was just as important—and we were outnumbered and outranked.

Today leadership positions are occupied by a greater percentage of women than ever. We are becoming more comfortable with the expanding definition of leadership that is carefully researched by Dr. Décosterd. She is perfectly placed to demonstrate how women over time have brought us to this point and what important traits these women possess. Her approach is astute and profound. Dr. Décosterd has developed an IDEA-based leadership model— the key traits being *intuitive* orientation, *directive* force, *empowering* intent, and *assimilative* nature—and gives us numerous methods for becoming more proficient in each area. She notes that the IDEA-based leadership model comes from "the true *complete* feminine perspective" found in the female socio-cultural patterns and can be followed by either sex to achieve lasting success.

In reading Dr. Décosterd's detailed description of the IDEA-based leader-ship model, I realized that it is the actual nature of women that has transformed leadership into meaning these things. I was struck by how much of my success could be directly attributed to using these key traits throughout my career—often secretly. Specifically, there was a corporate culture that frowned upon things like intuition as nonscientific, inconsequential, and soft. I remember a precise moment when my male colleagues and I were sitting at a conference table discussing a problem that all of them seemed not to understand. I had been listening for days and knew what to do instinctively. I used the words "I feel . . ." to explain my position. My boss quickly stated that "we are not paid for what we *'feel,'* we are paid for what we *think*!" I remember being a bit confused as to what the difference was—do none of these guys *feel* when they evaluate information with their brain? Mary Lou's insightful explanation of an intuitive orientation clarifies the importance of intuition once and for all. She systematically does the same for all four IDEA-based leadership traits.

Dr. Décosterd has carefully researched numerous dynamic, remarkable, influential, and successful women to demonstrate how their values, actions, and sense of purpose reflect these four key elements of leadership. I loved reading one story after another of inspiring women whose leadership touched my life and resonated what I believed to be true. We hear too little about these amazingly courageous and evolved women in our daily lives, and without this tribute to these superwomen, we may never have understood their important role in our collective story.

In these complex times, *How Women Are Transforming Leadership: Four Key Traits Powering Success* is a breath of fresh air. Dr. Décosterd has presented a timely and compelling argument for the feminine leadership perspective, stewardship, and balance. She is clear that our leaders must be proficient in using their right and left brains and the best of their masculine and feminine traits to become whole, wise individuals—and she leaves us with specific directives for women and for all leaders. With this insightful book, you will clearly understand these traits, their value to you personally, and how you can incorporate them into your leadership style and into your life to make real and lasting change.

Carla L. Picardi
Author of *The World According to YOU! . . .
How Our Choices Create It All*

ACKNOWLEDGMENTS

The first to be acknowledged are my family members, who have been a primary source of support and inspiration leading up to and during the writing. I am named after my two grandmothers, Mary and Lucy. My Grandma Mary worked in the family's business. What I remember most about Grandma Mary is her resilience, how she maintained her cool, and how she always seemed to look for the silver lining. Her daughter, my Aunt Claire, is to this day driven by nature and is where I believe much of my tenacity comes from.

My Grandma Lucy and I were inseparable. Mostly I recall her unconditional love and unusually progressive outlook within the context of a dramatically traditional existence. She passed away when I was 16. I only hope she knew just how important she was to me. I owe much of who I am to her and to her husband, my Grandpa Swift. When I think of the two of them together, I recall their deep and genuine affection for one another. They were the cutest of couples. I loved how attentive they were with each other, but more importantly how they respected each other's differences. What set them each apart is what they seemed to love most about the other. That image kindled my perspective of how men and women can and should live and work together as individuals and as leaders: through an appreciation for and blending of collective strong suits. My grandfather was a self-made success and as such embodied the American dream. It is from him I learned to aspire.

My mother and her sisters Toni and Laura are amazing. Seeing them together is like watching the best possible "feel good" movie. They joke. They make "stuff." They generate solutions to the problems of the world in a way that is refreshingly basic and remarkably wise. My sister Linda; my cousins Lisa, Karen, Kristen, and Jeanine; my sister-in-law Carol; and their girls Laura, Emily, Vianna, Ellen, Tara, and Nicole, Gina, and Sarah (my precious nieces) are a treasured female cohort. My brother Tony; sweet nephew Sam; Uncles Bob and Jim; cousins Mike, Bobby, Jimmy, and Pat; and their sons Ryan, Cole, Jimmy, and Patrick complete the Sodora family picture.

We lost our beloved cousin Billy when he was far too young. So much good can be said about Billy. He represents what I now think of when I envision a balanced leader. Billy's qualities afforded him the essence of individual drive infused with a stunning social conscience; accomplishment was only noteworthy for Billy if the greater group benefited as well.

My husband Jean-Pierre is my rock and one of the really "good guys" in work and in life. He is now retired from a successful executive leadership career. Those who worked for and with him no doubt feel that they were always in good hands. It is lovely to watch as my extraordinary step-daughters Patricia and Yasmine follow in their father's footsteps, Trish through her adventurous nature and Yasmine as the quintessential can-do leader. To my Swiss family—Marcel, Susi, Daniel and Lucas, Astrid, Peter, Tanja and Marco and of course, my dear mother- and father-in-law Erna and Paul—though far away, you are always close in thought. Also distant loved ones are my father Tony and my stepmom Bernice. Thank you both for your caring support. Last but far from least are my sweet puppies Max and Lilly. Lilly, you are your mother's daughter, and Maxie, you are mommy's little man.

Quite important to acknowledge are those who worked on the book itself. This is my third book with Debbie Carvalko, a most committed editor. Michelle Rooney is my right hand and left brain. Thank you, Michelle, for getting into the details and always being there as only you can. Denise Cantrell and Marilyn Rosskam were my second and third sets of eyes. Thank you both so very much—mostly thank you for your friendship. Thanks to Jackie Rogers for her research, and extra-special thanks to my most respected colleagues, mentors, and trusted friends Jerri Frantzve, Christine Troianello, Anita Augustine, and Debbie Himsel for providing the learned interviews and for your longer-term, invaluable personal and professional support. I was so very fortunate to have encouragement of a more personal nature during this project from always-there BFF Sue Spinella, from Donna Zulch (my role model for grace under fire), and from Lynnie, Barb, Kevin, Ri Ri, Donna and Don, Susanne and company, Frannie, Nancy and Peter, Carrie and John, Beth Ann, Kathy, and Katie.

Cynthia Davis introduced me to Carla Picardi, who wrote the book's fore-word. No wonder they are friends—they are both powerhouse women. Carla is a model leader and the absolute loveliest person. Carla, I sincerely thank you for taking the time to do this. Anyone who hasn't done so already must read Carla's book, *The World According to You! . . . How Our Choices Create It All*. It is spot on.

Those who took the time to provide endorsements to the book include Frances Grote, Joann Davis Brayman, Dr. Christopher Shoemaker, and the distinguished General Ann Dunwoody. Fran is an accomplished business leader and author. Her book *Fire in the Henhouse* is a wonderfully entertaining must-read as well. Joann Davis Brayman is a consummate marketing execu-tive and champion of women. Dr. Shoemaker is a global business leader and strategist and provided the much-appreciated male point of view. General Dunwoody recently retired from her most historic career in the military. It is a supreme honor to have had General Dunwoody, Fran, Joann, and Chris support the book.

Our clients at the Lead Life Institute deserve immeasurable tribute. We love what we do because we get to work day in and day out with impactful leaders who want nothing more than to make a difference. Over the years you have continued to shape our leadership views and have informed the book's model. Particular thanks to our women's leadership seminar attendees for powerful intensives together. Special thanks to clients who have shared specific stories and concerns relative to the gender leadership debate. Finally, acknowledgment goes out to *all* influential women, past, present, and still to come, whose accomplishments have and will continue to shape *how women* are *transforming leadership*!

CHAPTER 1

AN EVOLUTION OF INFLUENCE: WOMEN, LEADERSHIP, AND LIFE

Far away there in the sunshine are my highest aspirations. I may not reach them, but I can look up and see their beauty, believe in them, and try to follow where they lead.

—Louisa May Alcott[1]

SETTING THE TONE

Louisa May Alcott was born in Germantown, Pennsylvania, not far from where I live today. We both moved a fair amount, living and working in different places. We are authors, educators, and staunch supporters of equality for women. Alcott has long been an inspiration of mine and certainly one of the countless women in history whose influence and impact is felt today. I often wonder what it would have been like to forge a career back in Alcott's days—to be as accomplished as she at any point in time, let alone back then. Alcott was not only a famous writer but worked multiple jobs to contribute to the care of her family, including serving as a nurse during the Civil War.[2] I can only imagine that in whichever roles she assumed, she touched the lives of those around her and contributed immeasurably to how women were seen and valued.

When I take on a new challenge, I think of Alcott. Her perspective gives rise to momentum. I consider more the power inherent in striving and less, at least initially, what the end result will be. Success becomes possible in part by the potency of one's reach. This is true for anyone who aspires to do and be more, to succeed, and to attain new levels of accomplishment. It is especially true for women. As women, we have had to forge new ground, break existing molds, and set new parameters in order to make a mark. *How Women Are Transforming Leadership* is my third leadership book and, for me, the most important. It is certainly the one closest to my heart. It is a book about women—their inherent nature. It speaks to how women's intricacies contribute immeasurably to *humankind*. More to the point, it is a book that calls out the need for *women's ways* to be more directly infused into the manner in which those in power lead, not only for the advancement of women but for the survival and enrichment of society as a whole.

How Women Are Transforming Leadership is a candid, factual account of the plight of women as professionals, as leaders, and most importantly as proprietors of their own destiny. Women have had to fight each and every step of the way in order to assert their intellect and impact. As women continue to drive the movement for parity and rights, societies mature; men and women alike become more effective, evolved, and civilized. When women advance in their various personal and professional roles, the world is reshaped for the better. As women take on higher positional authority with more regularity and equality, the culture of leadership is altered, as is the very nature of success. Finally, as matriarchs, women enrich how people relate to one another personally, professionally, and fundamentally.

Given all of that, what can you expect from this book? *How Women Are Transforming Leadership* examines the leadership personas of successful women in order to call out their perspectives and practices. From that examination, you will more succinctly see how such methods are enhancing and necessary to leadership practices overall. The field of leadership is at a crossroads. If we look at the problems we face globally, whether economic, environmental, developmental, or social, we see corrections occurring—corrections that point to a need for changes in how we live, how we relate, how we progress, and hence how we lead. The complexities of our world show a broadening in literally everything we do and experience, while leadership continues to be constricted by dated ways.

One way to conceptualize this is through the lens of how leadership as an entity came to be. Leadership is not merely male dominated, it is male invented. The culture of leadership has grown from male-based thinking and acting and from a time in our evolution where certain premises made sense. The world was more primal, and we as people behaved in ways that were principally based on survival. As we evolved, everything around us grew to be more intricate and diverse. We moved from an existence-based world to one centered on advancement, yet our leadership culture remained largely unchanged. While virtually everything around us made strides, leadership held steadfast to its original state. From state-of-the-art technologies to something as once basic as a cupcake, we see sophistications that reflect the complexities of today. How we lead needs a more cutting-edge composition as well. Leadership needs the perspective of all who work within it accounted for within its fabric. We need to stop thinking about how women need to fit into leadership—to "join the club"—and instead think about how to make the club more representative of its total membership.

If we think about how diverse communication practices are today—for example, how social networking has changed the way we conduct business—we need ask ourselves, is a solely male-based leadership perspective enough to address these new ways of relating? Surely communication diversity is one of many arenas where feminine leadership proclivities are additive. If we think about resource constraints on businesses, wouldn't a feminine perspective for leveraging human capital be important? In my work as an executive coach to business leaders, I can assure you that a primary struggle of leaders today is how to deal more effectively with such people constraints. Their pain is mostly due to the fact that male-based leadership practices limit how this particular matter is viewed, positioned, and addressed. "The bigger the problem, the bigger the stick," is the current trend, meaning to put more pressure on folks to do what they need to do. This is not a solution. This is an overplayed hand in a downward-spiraling poker game.

Within the past several decades, we have seen mention in the leadership literature that the most effective leaders are the ones who act from more androgynous perspectives, those who integrate male and female values, strong suits, and styles into how they lead. The actual application of androgyny, though, gets mostly lip service from those in power. It is not taken as seriously as it should be. In order to be successful in today's world, leaders need a more gender-integrated leadership framework, one in which male and female inclinations are reflected. The patronizing and misguided impression that bringing women into the world of leadership is about helping women better acclimate to the existing male-based culture should be replaced with thinking that places women as true equals at the leadership table. This is no longer an assimilation issue. It is an imperative to correct a woefully stunted perspective. The aim here is to precisely call out the viable feminine leadership traits sorely needed in current, incomplete leadership practices. To that end, *How Women Are Transforming Leadership* makes those feminine traits explicit and therefore accessible for the conversation.

VENUS AND MARS DECONSTRUCTED

As we work to put men and women on the same leadership page, let's begin by calling out how Venus and Mars relate. Two constructs will be presented, one a female leadership inclination and one male. Both examples reflect a strong suit. Interestingly, the strong suits typically turn into overplayed strengths because of the way men and women tend to relate when they negatively feed off of each other. Put another way, because male and female leadership ways are not yet integrated, everyone's individual effectiveness is in jeopardy of being diminished.

On the female side, we turn to women's perspectives on learning. Women approach leadership and life through a learning lens. It isn't that men don't learn and value learning, but women view learning differently than men do. Men have been socialized to be goal directed, to win, and to achieve. Women have been socialized to master. Perhaps it stems from fairly primal roots—giving birth to a child, a fragile, helpless infant that you are trusted to protect and care for. If you make a mistake, the consequences can be grave. Women value getting it right, and they will do what it takes to ensure that they do. At work, that can translate to showing vulnerabilities, calling out what we don't know, or asking others for suggestions. It also means apologizing when things don't go the way we think they should have gone. Men can see this as a weakness, while women see it as a needed discussion point.

Now factor in women's current work-life circumstances. These often require that they manage multiple, rival roles. When you live in a world of constant juggling, it is hard to feel that you ever give anything the effort it deserves. Women have elevated multitasking to an art form and operate routinely with their attention pulled in different directions. When you function in such a manner day in and day out, it is understandable how doing so can leave one feeling discontented with the results. You come to believe that no one thing is done to *your* total satisfaction. It is also difficult to feel a sense of control, which is unnerving in itself.

To compensate and perhaps ease our internal unrest, we apologize. The apology is seemingly our way of saying, "I could have done it better if I had more time," but in leadership circles, it comes across as diminished power. Most of those around us never notice a problem with what we deliver; it is how we feel inside. Our overplayed apology, though, opens the door to an impression of self-effacement and perhaps of being less capable or less *in command.* There is an expression, "men apologize for their mistakes, women for their successes." "Great job on that presentation Sue," says Sue's boss. Sue's reply is, "I should have also brought in those figures from China." "How do you think the meeting went, Joan?" her peer inquires. "Next time I think I would have spent more time on the cost issues," she answers. Her coworker remarks, "Really? I thought the tone and outcome was more than we could have hoped for."

This reticent behavior conveys weakness, plain and simple, and frailty is not leaderlike. Women have a decided strength here—a focus on mastery, an openness to learning, and, more to the point, an ability to admit mistakes when appropriate, *sans* ego constraints. In order to be held in high leadership regard, women need to portray it as such. We need to reconcile our own inner demons and portray a resoundingly favorable side to the admirable trait of being mastery driven. Respond instead with statements such as, "Yes, thank you, the presentation seemed to be well received. Considering the discussion, perhaps next time, I could include some information about China for deeper understanding." Accept credit, honor what you did, and show that even more is possible.

With respect to the place of apologies in leadership, expressing a valid apology is a crucial aspect of leading. A legitimate apology can and should be leveraged as a formidable leadership trait. While women may be prone to apologizing unnecessarily, they also show great leadership facility when they appropriately accept responsibility for actual mistakes. This keen and courageous trait encourages a culture of learning in all those who surround such a leader. As such, a tone is set for open dialogue and healthy transparency. We become more able to accurately assess current circumstances, we demonstrate integrity and character, and we move our teams more effectively toward developing best practices. Lastly, when the person at the top aptly admits difficulty, it is just plain refreshing. It is humbling in a good way and by no means compromises the standing of a competent individual.

When I looked for an example of healthy contrition in a leader, a man actually came to mind. That man is President Obama. Perhaps the fact that the president was raised by a strong woman who was also an educated scholar helped nurture this leadership ability in him. Obama himself reports that his mother instilled straightforward values in him in addition to teaching him to have a distinct appreciation for learning. The president has in fact made public apologies at several critical junctures in his presidency. In early February 2009, former Democratic leader Tom Daschle stepped down from nomination as secretary of health and human services due to irregularities with his past tax filings. On February 3, 2009, on a CNN live interview with Anderson Cooper, when questioned about problems with Daschle's appointment, Obama replied, "I think I screwed up." When was the last time we heard a prominent leader say that? The exchange with Anderson Cooper went as follows:

Cooper: Do you feel you messed up in letting it get this far?

Obama: Yes, I think I made a mistake and I told Tom that. I take responsibility for the appointees.

Cooper: What was your mistake—letting it get this far or should you have pulled it earlier?

Obama: I think my mistake is not in selecting Tom originally because I think nobody was better qualified to deal with both the substance and policy of health care. He understands it as well as anybody, but also the politics which is going to be required to actually get it done. But I think ultimately I campaigned on changing Washington and bottom up politics and I don't want to send a message to the American people that there are two sets of standards, one for powerful people and one for the ordinary folks who are working every day and paying their taxes.

Cooper: Do you think you've lost some of your moral high ground you set for yourself on Day 1?

Obama: Well I think this was a mistake. I think I screwed up and I take responsibility for it and we're gonna make sure we fix it so it doesn't happen again.[3]

Stated simply and directly, with no defensiveness or excuses, the president took full responsibility, admitted his mistake, and walked us through his learning. Openly noting miscalculations or acknowledging that there is room for improvement is a sound leadership trait. It is something we need to see more of in our leaders in all walks of leadership life. Traditional (male-based) leadership views would not agree. Obama's opponents used his apologies as a way to discredit him; they called him weak for apologizing. While the over-apologizing described at the outset of this section can and will undermine a leader's image, the justified apology is a solid and necessary leadership trait. Those who consider it otherwise are revealing shortcomings in their own ability to understand and respond to the complexities of our world as well as insecurities and credibility gaps with respect to who they are as people.

To set the proper tone for what is to follow, let's agree that leaders (women in particular) reading this who are prone to the overapology will agree to *stop apologizing* when it isn't called for and set a strong feminine example by continuing to do so when it is. Think of unneeded contrition as a self-inflicted wound that only serves to set you back. When you feel an apology coming on, ask yourself this: Did I really do something wrong? If so, by all means apologize. If not, consider how you need to react instead in order to be seen as positive, affirming, and influential. Here's an example that can serve as a model for you.

You come rushing into a meeting with a team. You are the project leader. Looking frazzled, you scurry to your seat and say, "So sorry to be late." The fact is you are the last to arrive, but you aren't late.

Now rewind. Instead, as you head down the hall to the meeting, you take note of the fact that you feel a bit harried. Stop, take a deep breath, and collect yourself. Think of the one or two things you intend to come away with from today's meeting. Put on a confident face, walk into the room calmly, and say, "How is everyone? It's good to be here." That is all you need to do.

On the other hand, if you are someone who doesn't yet see the leadership value of openly learning from one's mistakes, agree to at least consider that, given the intricacies of most leadership challenges and demands, you may need to rethink things. The nature of the apology as a leadership strong suit or impediment is one example of the opportunities we have for productive gender-assimilated leadership discussions. It also clearly elucidates one reason for the existing divide.

The second construct is about men and competition. Traditional male-based leadership perspectives see competing as the path to success. Winning is supreme, and in order to win you have to compete. All of those things are true. We compete with ourselves to become better. We compete with others to win at sports, in business, and in life. Competition is healthy; it breeds resilience and perseverance, and it pushes us beyond what we thought possible. In its most effective form, competition instills a sense of purpose. It engenders drive and enables us to transcend limits and constraints. Men were historically reared to see competition as their first line of defense. The Darwinian premise of survival of the fittest sets a certain tone for how one should act if one hopes to endure and thrive. Overcompeting, though, is a detriment.

Overcompeting can cause precipitous mistakes and, at times, colossal failure. It prevents necessary collaboration and can close us off to listening and learning. Overcompeting makes it difficult if not impossible to consider mutually beneficial outcomes. It can cut us off to learning and thus cause us to be blind-sided as we are fixated. It is somewhat like shutting down one's peripheral vision or driving without side- or rear-view mirrors. Your car may outrun the pack, but it may also be hit by something unexpected. An overly competitive mindset causes leaders to dig in once they have a path forward in mind. It may even make one overcommit, to stretch for targets that are unrealistic or even unnecessary, just for the sake of the game. The leader can, as a result, become closed off to any input that contradicts the committed course. He or she may not see warning signs of danger ahead, no matter how blatant. Mistakes and errors in judgment are marginalized. Leaders who overcompete also tend to resist anything new or different. Change of any nature can make them feel that they are losing control or giving up ground. In response, they dig in and they pull in; they resist.

Just as today's context provokes women to overplay their leadership propensities, the same is true for men. Today's business climate has grown more fiercely competitive, more survival-based, and this provokes some to overcompete all the more. Financial collapse and the Wall Street–driven immediacy of demands have made futures more tenuous for everyone. Leaders, especially those at the top, are pushing harder and harder to impress more pointedly. The "new old boys' club" seems to stand for tenacity to the hundredth power. There is less room at the top, so they want to deliver the impossible in order to secure their spot. The only way they may see to do this is to overcompete. The more they overcompete, the more they resist change, especially when it comes to the foundations of how one should lead. Such core resistance makes feminine leadership inclusion difficult if not impossible. Overcompeting can and does make men view women coming into their leadership turf as threats. They may outwardly say the politically correct thing (and many may actually believe it)—that they support diversity in the workplace—but there is a more insidious force at work here. That force is culturally imbedded resistance.

Resistance is inevitable in all change movements. The status quo fights long and hard to retain its position. When confronted with change, the natural response is to focus more on what you stand to lose rather than to consider the upside. More importantly, stress can cause us to unknowingly become even more rigid and ingrained. We become entrenched in our thoughts and actions, and, as a result, the inclination is to do what we know best. In this case, men react to their stressors by overcompeting, which leads to greater resistance. Because stress is all around us, this cycle needs to be called out in order to break it. When stressed, we are prone to believe that the soundest way to address our problems is to stick to what we know. We retreat to our comfort zones. Doing what we know and what we are best at seems the right path. Women, though, have taken precisely these most arduous moments to proclaim that they want a new leadership path chartered. In doing so, women are attempting to influence men at precisely the times when men are most set in their ways. This is not a great recipe for progress.

Consider the current nature of U.S. politics. In the past decade, we have seen overcompeting at its worst. In spite of escalating troubled times, Democrats and Republicans alike held firm to their ideals. Each faction behaved more and more in self-serving ways in order to win. Think about trying to change the minds of a staunch Democrat or Republican today. Overcompeting makes this extremely difficult. Consequently, the country is left at a disadvantage. The potential collective leadership know-how of the parties cannot be brought to bear to solve our problems. Instead, each works to undermine the other, obscure good policies and sound thinking, and obstruct progress. Overcompeting has become so intense in Washington that every year is an election year—the politicians literally never stop running for office. And while many are bright, good people who know better intellectually, the circumstance is too entrenched. Appropriate competition will always have its star place in leadership. Overcompeting needs to stop.

The time has come for men and women to come together as peer leaders and have thoughtful, provocative, and germane discussions about the future direction of leadership. The questions we need to be asking ourselves are these:

What is it that makes a leader truly great?

What do we all agree on?

What are our most pressing leadership challenges?

What do we collectively bring to address these challenges?

What isn't working?

What are our sources of contention?

What has history told us?

What can we infer about the future?

What can we learn from each other?

What do we agree on as our starting point?

How Women Are Transforming Leadership attempts to provide, no pun intended, a pregnant pause (a curious term, isn't it?) so that we can begin to think through the answers to these and other pertinent questions. It seeks to afford readers time to consider the consequences of our current lives and circumstances, along with the opportunity for measured reflection regarding the future of leadership. Through the stories, models, and concepts that follow, we can begin to reassess how to work together toward more gender-assimilated leadership ways.

How Women Are Transforming Leadership has three distinct components. It includes a tribute to influential women. Though no one book can adequately capture all of what women have contributed, a sizable number of noteworthy women throughout history and up to the present day will be referenced. The book calls attention to their impact, and more importantly, demonstrates how women have and are continuing to shape modern-day leadership styles and perspectives.

The second charge of the book is to caption women's leadership cornerstones. *How Women Are Transforming Leadership* identifies the manner in which successful women of the past and present lead and how their values, actions, and sense of purpose meld to form critical elements of leadership. Four key traits are identified—traits that, when applied to the way one leads, can have far-reaching business and societal impacts. The final aim of the book is to provide a roadmap for anyone with leadership responsibilities—executives, bosses, teachers, public figures, parents, coaches, team and project leaders, men and women alike—to easily leverage the book's four key traits and thus enhance their impact and effectiveness in work and in life. To set the tone, we begin with some interesting and perhaps not-so-well-known facts about women and their accomplishments.

DID YOU KNOW ...

Harriet Tubman

Harriet Tubman was a well-known black civil rights activist whose efforts resulted in the freeing of over 300 slaves, but did you know that Harriet Tubman had a bounty on her for $40,000? Tubman's civil rights efforts were truly remarkable. Forty thousand dollars was a colossal sum of money in her time and certainly reflects the level of threat she was perceived to be by the status quo. Let's trace her story. Tubman was born in Maryland in 1820. Her parents were slaves, and she herself began working in the fields at the age of seven. She was said to be willful, independent, and unusually physically resilient. When she was a young teenager, she was struck on the head for protecting another slave from punishment. The injury was so forceful that the young Harriet had recurring and often debilitating symptoms. Still she pressed on. Years later, Tubman performed her most daring exploit. In 1857, she secured a wagon. Armed with a rifle, Tubman set out to bring her elderly parents along with hundreds of other slaves to freedom. Tubman accomplished her mission, and not one individual under her care was captured.[4] Tubman possessed exceptional courage, compassion, character, and determination. How exciting it would be to know a woman like Harriet Tubman, to work alongside her or to be led by her! One would certainly feel in good hands.

Eleanor Roosevelt

Did you know that Eleanor Roosevelt had an FBI file that was more than 3,000 pages long? Perhaps more readily known was that John Foster Dulles, President Eisenhower's secretary of state, reportedly remarked that the former first lady was "more subversive and dangerous than Moscow." A former first lady with stunning human rights accomplishments was seen by some as more subversive and dangerous than Moscow? Is Dulles's perspective that of a healthy skeptic, or is it, rather, more one of overly competitive, resistant thinking? Roosevelt's professional life includes work to support health-care reform, day care, youth groups, unemployment, and civil rights. She was a syndicated newspaper columnist and stood strong against the influential, but discriminatory, Daughters of the American Revolution for their discriminatory beliefs and practices. She was a U.S. delegate to the United Nations, chaired the United Nations'

Commission on Human Rights, and had a part in drafting the Declaration of Human Rights. Her last professional contribution was as a member of the Commission on the Status of Women during the Kennedy administration.[5]

Today, Eleanor Roosevelt is thought of as one of the most important women of the twentieth century. Her infamous quote, "No one can make you feel inferior without your consent," is an awe-inspiring message to live by when we come face to face with self-doubt. Hers is a leadership message to motivate and to instill perseverance. Roosevelt embodied a subtle yet potent power: when confronted with opposition or with those acting in ways contrary to what she believed in, she simply stayed her course. She taught us how to lead and influence by counterexample, modeling the opposite of those behaving badly as a way to point out the more admirable and effective path. What I have learned from Roosevelt is the importance of modeling in leadership and how to hold onto my power—not to give it away or become subverted by those with perhaps nothing more than a louder horn.

Margaret Sanger

Did you realize that it wasn't until 1965 that the U.S. Supreme Court struck down the last state law prohibiting the personal use of contraceptives, and that a nurse, Margaret Sanger, led that movement? Sanger's quest was for women to have safe, reliable, and legal means for preventing pregnancies. Sanger died in 1966, not long after the Supreme Court ruling. She began the birth control movement in the United States in 1912.[6]

Women Nobel Prize Laureates

How many Nobel Prize recipients can you recall who are women? The number is 43. Marie Curie was awarded a Nobel Prize twice, once in 1903 in physics and again in 1911 in chemistry. She was the first female recipient. A total of 549 Nobel Prizes have been awarded in all between 1903 and 2012. Of the 43 female recipients, 1 woman won in economics, 2 in physics, 4 in chemistry, 10 in physiology and medicine, 15 in peace, and 12 in literature.[7] We hail the accomplishments of these admirable women, but the overall numbers are telling and disappointing.

Martha McSally

Do you know who Martha McSally is? Martha McSally was the first female fighter pilot. She went on to become the first woman in the United States to fly a combat mission in a fighter aircraft and the first woman to command a combat aviation squadron. McSally accumulated more than 2,600 flying hours, including 325 combat hours in Iraq and Afghanistan. In 1995, McSally flew her first combat mission into Iraq to enforce the United Nations' "no fly-zone." She flew two additional tours in the Middle East in support of Operation Southern Watch. McSally also served as an A-10 instructor pilot. She was later appointed legislative fellow and advised Senator John Kyl of Arizona on a variety of defense, international security, terrorism, and cybersecurity issues. This assignment included a tour in Saudi Arabia, where McSally was responsible for combat search-and-rescue operations for all coalition aircraft over Iraq and Afghanistan. This assignment occurred during the 9/11 attacks, and McSally was part of a leadership group planning the initial air campaign in Afghanistan. Her military awards include the Defense Superior Service Medal, the Bronze Star, and numerous Air Medals for combat missions and for her leadership skill.

McSally is also the first uniformed officer to sue the Department of Defense. In 2001, when McSally was on mission in Saudi Arabia, she had to wear culturally appropriate female attire (that is, cover up her face) and stay on base while stationed there. She objected on the grounds that she was a service officer and had an appropriate uniform to wear in that regard. She also felt that as an officer, she should have the same freedom of movement as her male counterparts as she was, in fact, a member of that cohort. At that time, she was the highest-ranking female fighter pilot in the Air Force. Eventually, Congress approved legislation that prohibited anyone in the military from requiring or encouraging servicewomen to put on abayas in Saudi Arabia or to use taxpayers' money to buy them.[8] Think about the implications of what was expected of this military commander. She was on the one hand expected to lead air troops into battle and pilot jet aircraft into enemy territory, yet she had to behave in the most subservient of manners while not on missions. While one must respect the culture of a country, McSally was there as part of a different cultural group, a cohort within which she deserved to be an equal.

Boudicca

Did you know that the word *bodacious* came from the accomplishments of a Celtic heroine? The word *bodacious,* meaning bold or remarkable in an outrageous sort of way, came from Queen Boudicca of the Iceni tribe, whose people inhabited the eastern edge of England during the first century CE. Boudicca was reported as being physically imposing, a tall, large-boned woman with waist-long red hair and a booming voice. She was married to King Prasutagus, who shared his legacy with the Roman Emperor Nero. When King Prasutagus died in 60 CE, the Romans committed an unscrupulously brutal act. They beat Boudicca, raped her two daughters, and stole the family's half of their inheritance. In retaliation, the brazen, fiery-haired Queen, mother, and widow led a revolt in which the Romans were nearly defeated. As such, Boudicca followed Cleopatra to become the second woman in history to stand tall against the mighty Romans. Her actions are renowned in England to this day, and a statue of Boudicca remains near Westminster Pier in London as a tribute to her heroism.[9] This is the woman I want on my side in times of trouble.

Wu Chao

Finally, did you know that in 690 CE China had a woman ruler? Empress Wu Chao, also known as Wu Hou or Wu Zetien, was the only woman in the nation's history to hold the throne in her own name. Wu Chao was self-appointed empress of China from 690 to 705 CE during the T'ang dynasty. Additionally, she led the nation for 23 years prior while her husband, Emperor Gaozong, was too ill to do so. During the years that Wu Chao stepped in for her husband, she not only saw to matters of state but was the self-proclaimed commander and chief of the military as well.

Empress Chao was known for being as altruistic as she was ruthless. Her reign was thus marked by positive social reforms and deliberate, cunning, and coldblooded attacks on those who opposed her. During Empress Wu's time in power, the country's economy thrived and the people enjoyed peace and harmony. She replaced the governing caste system with appointments based on qualifications. She promoted culture and the arts and the develop-ment of Buddhism throughout China. As Wu Chao secured and retained her position, she systematically eliminated anyone who got in her way. Wu Chao resorted to framing some for crimes they did not commit, to poisonings and slayings, and to ordering the annihilation of mass numbers of her resist-ers. While this side of Wu Chao could be characterized as malevolent, another way to view it is as iconoclastic. The empress set out to challenge the self-serving ways of governing and to instead secure rights for the people. When one's adult life begins as Wu Chao's did—at the age of 13, she was chosen as concubine to two emperors—the times demand perhaps desperate measures to secure even the most basic of human rights.[10] Wu Chao's gender, coupled with when and where she held power, is a testament to how determined, accomplished, and savvy a leader she was.

DOUBLE STANDARD/DOUBLE BIND

These stories and facts are interesting historical vignettes. All of the women mentioned thus far were activists on some level; they had to be in order to realize their personal and professional goals. Harriet Tubman and Eleanor Roosevelt were viewed as threats by those in power because of the change they sought to bring about in how the oppressed were treated. Margaret Sanger's accomplishment calls to attention how in the not-so-distant past women were not able to make basic and fundamental choices that decidedly impacted their life choices and professional reach. With the pace at which progress is made today on so many fronts (we wait impatiently as it takes *seconds* for the Internet to reach a site), it is difficult to imagine that less than 50 years ago safe and reliable birth-control methods were not available to women. The Nobel Prize numbers are disappointing. Roughly 12 percent of recipients to date are women. On the other hand, Martha McSally's accomplishments demonstrate what parity should look like.

Lastly, we learned of two rulers—Queen Boudicca, a fearless warrior, and Wu Chao, a formidable Empress—leaders whose contentious acts were rooted in the best of leadership values. Both Boudicca and Wu Chao sought to avenge wrongdoings, hold others accountable, and promote the holistic development of a people. Boudicca acted with ferocity to right a wrong, and Wu Chao saw her high position as that of a public servant. She thwarted those who saw power as self-serving. For her, positional authority was about what stature allows one to do for others.

All of these women acted in aggressive ways. All were tough in their own right. Robust behavior, in whatever form, when coming from a woman in a position of leadership brings to light the final foundational point to be made. That point is the matter of the *double standard/double bind*. Women continue to be held back as leaders by the simple fact that formidable behavior is perceived differently when it comes from a man versus a woman. This *double standard* speaks directly to the point made earlier that leadership is male-invented, that it stems from male-based social values. When a man acts forcefully, society sees it as positive; when a woman does, most men and still many women continue to perceive it as negative. When women leaders are bellicose, they can be typed as out of control, while that very same behavior coming from a male counterpart would be hailed. Consider honestly how many of us would react to a *bodacious* woman as our superior. Consider also what it would be like for a man versus a woman to have a Wu Chao–like boss. Might there be differences in how men and women would react? Might there also be differences in how any of us would perceive an imposing female boss versus a man who behaves in exactly the same manner? These are all interesting questions to ponder.

Here is yet another thought to consider. Both Boudicca and Wu Chao acted in seemingly violent ways. What labels would be assigned to Boudicca and Wu Chao by men versus women? Might more women tend to see Boudicca and Chao as perhaps strong, heroic, liberating, and justified, when many men might characterize these leaders in less favorable lights? In my work with women leaders, a common complaint continues to be that they are not able to lead from an equal playing field—that their more forceful leadership behavior is too often perceived negatively. As a result, women don't always know or understand what is expected of them; hence the *double bind*. "If I confront, I'm too pushy, and if I don't, I'm weak" is the usual conundrum. Compounding the matter further, the rules seem to change as roles, bosses, and organizational cultures change. Regardless of the context, though, behaviors such as raising one's voice, confronting directly and openly, or laying down the law with subordinates is more often than not more keenly scrutinized for women, whereas men engaging in the same behavior are given much more free reign.

This double standard/double bind is a fundamental indicator of the resistance that persists in bringing women into leadership's social fabric. Even when women "act as men," trying to measure up to supposed leadership standards, they are shortchanged. Only when we agree to eradicate this double standard/double bind, and do so openly and with accountability, will we make the headway needed. What would that look like? It would look like this:

1. Leaders *from the top down* would have to participate in training and open discussions about double-standard/double-bind issues and be held formally accountable through their performance measures to address instances of it appropriately.
2. Double standard/double bind behavior would need to be *explicitly (and legally) treated as a form of harassment*, making it an accepted part of a company's formal compliance process, meaning that it is publically wrong and those who engage in it are in jeopardy. We need to apply the same premises we have in place for sexual harassment to double-standard/double-bind issues, seeing it as a form of gender-based leadership harassment, which in fact, it is.
3. Leaders *from the top down* would have to stop insisting that double standard/double bind is an old, played-out complaint that has been addressed. It hasn't. It is alive and well, operating freely in most companies today in some form.
4. *All leaders* should be formally groomed to act with backbone and to set firm limits through uniformly acceptable and clearly articulated behaviors and parameters.
5. Leaders need to be seen as *genderless* in this and all regards. There needs to be one yardstick and one dashboard to measure leaders' efficacy by. No extraneous factors such as double standard/double bind can enter into play.

As we continue with our review of influential women, we see examples of how women have pushed back on double standard/double bind in order to make their impact.

GLOBAL LEADERS OF THE PAST

Perhaps Wu Chao and Queen Boudicca were more male-like in their behavior and demeanors as rulers. Here are several additional stories of global women rulers throughout history who played to their feminine strengths, beginning with none else than Cleopatra.

Cleopatra

Cleopatra stands as Queen Boudicca's counterpart, the only other woman in history to nearly defeat the Romans. The Roman regime feared Cleopatra for her political power, but there was another force at work contributing to their unrest with the queen. Cleopatra's successes could, in effect, have also unwittingly contributed to the empowerment of Roman women. Egyptian women were apparently more liberated than their Roman counterparts. They could choose their own husbands and pursue political power. Roman women were bound to domestic loyalty, chastity, and menial work. As Cleopatra's rising power threatened the Roman Empire, her opponents rallied against her by emphasizing her foreignness as an Egyptian and portraying her as a greedy harlot.

My cousin Laura did a paper on Cleopatra in her 2009 Sex and Gender in Greco-Roman Antiquity class. Laura's perspective is worth noting. She writes,

> Cleopatra was not actually Egyptian. In fact, she descended from Alexander the Great's General Ptolemy of Macedon (which was part of ancient Greece). While, granted, Greece is not Rome, Cleopatra was not nearly as foreign to the Romans as she was presented; she certainly was not very "oriental," as others who have written of her suggest. I believe that the fact that Cleopatra was so nearly Roman made her all the more frightening to them. That would explain why they were so desperate to pass her off as a foreigner: They did not want their own women to emulate her as a paragon of the empowerment of women. By criticizing her as foreign and power-hungry, Cleopatra's personality is cast in a negative light. Her power and achievements are no longer legitimate accomplishments, but rather are acts of shame.[11]

Laura's points are well taken. The fact remains that Cleopatra was just as accomplished as any powerful male ruler of her time. Her sexuality and ethnicity, though, became the focus as a means of discrediting her leadership impact. Regarding Cleopatra, the prevailing inference was that the only possible way for a woman to achieve what she had was through seduction. Furthermore, she should not be trusted because she was "not one of us," when in fact she nearly was. Surely brains, political savvy, and leadership acumen could not be at work—only sex, alien nature, and improper motives. What seems more interesting is the thought of Cleopatra as both an accomplished ruler and societal liberator. All things considered, while she did sexually conquer two of the most powerful men in the Roman Empire, Queen Cleopatra did seem capable of much more than a good time.

Catherine the Great

Catherine the Great ruled Russia from 1762 to 1796, during which time she was devoted to cultural and educational reform. As such, she was seen as a progressive intellectual. Germane to the topic at hand, she founded Russia's first school for girls and promoted the education of women in general. Much like Cleopatra, historical depictions of Catherine focus on her social and sexual proclivities, yet in actuality she was a brilliant thinker and diplomat and, overall, an influential leader. One could liken the skewing of attention away from leadership acumen to Catherine's social qualities to processes sadly still operating today, when during the 2008 U.S. presidential campaign there was far too much attention paid to what the formidable candidate Hilary Clinton wore rather than to the might of her message. I hardly recall a single time when mention was made of a male candidate's attire. This level of disempowering chatter is so deeply ingrained and insidious that it will only stop when we force it to.

Back to Catherine, one area of justified criticism regarding her leadership was perhaps her lack of attention to the common people. She seemed to find them off-putting. But do we see this as a shortcoming of Catherine because she was a woman—that it is unladylike to lack empathy? In Catherine's defense, it should be noted that the reforms she put into place in both education and for the economy, along with the scholarly thinking she fostered, paved the way for broader societal reform on all fronts. So perhaps she wasn't unconcerned with the poor after all. Though she led from a distance, she nonetheless had all of her peoples' interests at heart. Additionally, her accomplishments in foreign affairs were said to be exceptional, positioning Russia for the power it was to become.[12] The diplomatic skills that Catherine was noted for reflect her keen assimilative nature, an inherently feminine trait.

The Queens of England

Three leading queens of England include Queen Elizabeth I, Queen Victoria, and the currently reigning queen, Elizabeth II. Queen Elizabeth I ruled from 1558 to 1603. She was noted for ruling with absolute authority, yet she also led through maternal compassion for which her people named her "Good Bess." Good Bess was yet another female ruler who was thought of as a consummate diplomat. Throughout her reign, Queen Elizabeth commanded respect and loyalty from her people and was revered in matters of foreign affairs.[13]

Queen Victoria reigned for 64 years and was credited with bringing stature to both England and to the royals. Her namesake Victorian Era was a time of noteworthy industrial, economic, and cultural advancement for Great Britain. She had nine children, this would seem a reasonable path! My personally favorite historical point about the queen is what she said at age 11 when she reported, "I see I am nearer to the throne than I thought. I will be good." She indeed took the throne at the young age of 18 with confidence and independence. During her reign, there were seven attacks on her life, which she reportedly handled with great resolve.[14] I have a dear friend named Victoria who is both regal and assured. I see now where she gets it from.

The present-day Queen Elizabeth II is fascinating to me. She became queen in 1952, following the death of her father and during a time of political upheaval. Forty British colonies were granted sovereignty, and Northern Ireland was in unrest. Her role, while symbolic, was then and continues to be critical to the unity and continuity of the nation's heritage. She embodies what a British royal is meant to be and, in that sense, has been a selflessly fixed public servant.[15] If one thinks of how the world has changed during her reign, hers is a keen *assimilation* of the old world to a new one with effective consideration of her position and station. When one thinks of this queen, leadership descriptors that come to mind are *disciplined, unshaken, controlled,* and *astute.*

Rulers of the East

What do Golda Meir, Megawati, and Indira Gandhi have in common? They were each the first female head of government in their respective nations; all three were progressives; and all led, intensely opposed, during Byzantine times.

Golda Meir

Golda Meir was the first and still the only female prime minister of Israel. She was also the third female prime minister globally and the first to be called "Iron Lady," a name most think of as ascribed originally to Margaret Thatcher. Meir's resolve could be seen in how she led internally as well as how she was able to respond to acts of aggression against Israel itself. In 1972 at the Olympic Games, Israel's athletes were killed, and in 1973 a surprise attack led by Egypt and Syria on Israel's holy day of Yom Kippur ignited the Arab-Israeli War. Meir led her nation well through both critical times. Meir's view was that the strengthening of Israel as an advanced and developed democracy was crucial to its survival and position in the world. In spite of Meir's formidable resolve and the tumultuous positioning of Israel with respect to its Arab neighbors, her hope was for a civil coexistence. Meir's ability to reconcile these disparate circumstances and to act from both resolve and diplomacy marks the doubly complex leader that she was. It was because of her keen twofold skill that she was regarded as a vastly influential leader within the Middle East.[16]

Indira Gandhi

Indira Gandhi became the third prime minister of India, one of the most populated countries in the world, following her father's death in 1966. Though no relation to Mahatma Gandhi, she and her family were tied to the infamous civil rights leader in mission and principles. At the time that Indira Gandhi assumed office, India was facing considerable turmoil. A week prior to Gandhi's inauguration, the war between India and Pakistan reignited. She was also confronting a serious drought that had plagued India for two years, causing extreme food shortages and a devastating economic crisis. To make matters worse, her long-reigning political party lost control in Congress. During Gandhi's entire time in power she faced fierce, persistent political opposition—she representing the liberal view, the conservatives against her. She held her seat until 1977 and then won it back again in 1979. Gandhi was eventually assassinated in her home in 1984 by members of her own security force.[17]

What has been said about her leadership is that it was both a massive success and a colossal failure. Gandhi's success was in her determination to move India as a democratic nation. She formidably battled religious extremism with heroic fervor. She wanted nothing more than to improve the quality of life for her people and did whatever she could to make improvements on that front. Her failure was the result of the sheer magnitude of what she was taking on. This newly independent nation was riddled with internal struggles. The rivals she faced at home and abroad were pronounced. Still she fought hard, literally to the end.

Megawati

Megawati Sukarnoputri is the daughter of Sukarno, who was the first president of Indonesia. Megawati was Indonesia's fifth president and the first

Muslim female head of a modern national state. Her time in office ran from 2001 to 2004. In 2004, Megawati was in the top 10 of *Forbes*'s "100 Most Powerful Women" list. Her father had nine wives—an interesting side note. Megawati herself went from being a privileged housewife to a political figure. Her background and partisan views made her a threat to the existing regime, but she managed to garner enough popular support to oust her opponents and eventually become president. She was viewed by the people as honest and admirable. Her ruling emphasis was both basic and noble—to fight against the exploitation of the people and promote the continued development of democracy in Indonesia, a nation formerly under totalitarian rule.[18] While some historians suggest that Megawati was passive and only got where she did due to her father's former position, this was hardly the case. She was in fact what is referred to in the leadership literature as one who leads quietly—a leader who rules through relationships, collaborative discussion, and low-key yet empowering influence. Her style was well suited to the current state of affairs in Indonesia—exactly what the country needed at the time. Megawati's emphasis was on evolving her nation to one of shared administration. In that sense, it is moving to think of what Megawati accomplished with a softer, yet potent, touch.

For all of these great rulers and royals, it took supreme vision to direct their efforts and to decide where to seat themselves with respect to the contributions of their reign. Fortunately they had the benefit of women's fundamental and inherent *intuitive orientation*, a primary key feminine trait, to guide them.

THE WOMEN'S RIGHTS MOVEMENT

One could easily make the case that every leadership contribution by a woman both now and throughout time has been part of the women's rights movement. This segment looks more specifically at those women for whom women's rights was their primary focus.

Grassroots Women

> We women suffragists have a great mission—the greatest mission the world has ever known. It is to free half of the human race, and through that freedom, to save the rest.
>
> —Emiline Pankhurst[19]

When we think of the women's suffrage movement, we look to the late 1800s and into the early 1900s. Names such as Emiline Pankurst, Susan B.

Anthony, Elizabeth Cady Stanton, Carrie Chapman Catt, Mary Garret Hay, and Alice Paul come to mind. The above quote by one of those pioneers, *Emiline Pankurst*, is telling in several respects. Pankurst expresses vividly what no doubt any woman of contribution before her felt on some level: that the gender power and influence imbalance was neither rational nor in our best interest as a people. Interesting to note is that the British militant Pankurst was perhaps the most deliberately violent in her pursuits; she believed that radical means were needed to get the attention of her oppressors. Pankhurst's bold moves are thought to have done just that and to have given rise to the work that was to follow by women in the United States and in India. Well done, Emiline!

In the United States, *Elizabeth Cady Stanton* and *Susan B. Anthony* initiated the women's rights movement. Of their partnership Stanton wrote,

> In writing we did better work together that either could do alone. While she is the slow and analytical in composition, I am rapid and synthetic. I am the better writer, she the better oritic. She supplied the facts and statistics, I the philosophy and rhetoric, and together we made arguments which have stood unshaken by the storms of 30 long years: arguments no man has answered.[20]

What we see in this passage is the manner in which women combine forces, work collaboratively, and willingly share credit. It is part of women's communal nature and how they naturally empower others. Along those lines, it is interesting to note that the first four Nobel Prizes were awarded to women between 1903 and 1911, two to Marie Curie, a French citizen of Polish decent; one to Bertha von Suttner, the Austrian pacifist and novelist; and one to Selma Lagerlof, the progressive, world-traveled Swedish fiction writer. These deserving recipients were no doubt spurring suffragists everywhere. The U.S. women's movement reached a pivotal milestone during this precise time period. *Carrie Chapman Catt, Mary Garret Hay*, and *Alice Paul* are credited for the 1920 passage of the 19th Amendment finally granting women the right to vote. Women's *empowering intent* is yet another of the key feminine traits to be discussed at greater length.

Black Women's Dual Impact

Black women who fought for civil rights had to bear the dual burden of ethnic and gender oppression. Theirs was a unique vantage point, and they had a potent fury to drive them. In addition to aforementioned Harriet Tubman, women such as Mary McLeod, Sojourner Truth, Rosa Parks, and Ella Baker represent key contributions to humankind made by women of color during the civil rights movement. Their accomplishments will be forever cherished. For example, many say the modern civil rights movement began on December 1, 1955, when *Rosa Parks*, an ordinary seamstress in Montgomery, Alabama, refused to give up her seat on a bus to a white passenger. She was arrested for her brave act and later quoted as saying, "The only thing that bothered me was that we waited so long to make this protest." A young local pastor, Dr. Martin Luther King Jr., touched by Parks's act, aligned with her to form the Montgomery Improvement Association, whose first order of business was the boycott of the city-owned bus company. Their boycott lasted for 382 days, received international attention, and led to a Supreme Court decision that outlawed racial segregation on all public transportation.[21]

Looking at the life and work of Parks in greater detail, we see her for the transformational exemplar that she was. Parks's activism began long before her famous bus incident. It was her life mission to end racial inequality. As a child raised in the Deep South, she lived in fearful times. She made a conscious decision as a young woman not to be immobilized by her fear. Instead, she opted to learn what she could and use that knowledge to guide her in prudent action. She and her husband were vocal and devoted National Association for the Advancement of Colored People (NAACP) members, attuned to their community and working tirelessly to improve the lives of those around them. Their advances came from small, progressive steps. Though a graduate of Alabama State Teachers College, Parks only found work as a maid and seamstress, but teaching was in her blood. The bus incident presented an opportunity, and Parks took it. Her long life of service to a cause was immortalized when at the age of 75 she opened the Rosa and Raymond Parks Institute for Self-Development in Detroit, Michigan. She published her first book in 1994, *Quiet Strength: The Faith, the Hope, and the Heart of a Woman Who Changed a Nation.* Parks passed away in 2005.[22]

Sojourner Truth, an abolitionist and speaker, was noted as saying, "If a woman want any rights more than they've got, why don't they just take them and not be talking about it?"[23] Truth's speaking centered on the connection between the deprivation of slaves and women's rights. Prominent educator *Mary McLeod Bethune* started the National Council for Negro Women and organized a school for girls in 1904 that grew into a respected African American university. Bethune became the university's president and, later, a member of President Franklin Roosevelt's Black Cabinet.[24] If we look for the woman behind the movement, we would find *Ella Baker*. An activist, organizer, and fierce proponent of human rights, Baker was the true embodiment of leadership empowerment. She was less concerned with following leaders per se and more about encouraging the voice and spirit of all connected to a cause.

Modern-Day Heroines—To Name a Few

Those of the modern day who have advanced the rights for women might include diverse figures such as Billy Jean King, Gloria Steinem, Princess Diana, Mother Theresa, and Georgia O'Keeffe. *Billy Jean King's* pursuit of pay parity for women athletes peaked when she defeated Bobby Riggs in a highly sensationalized event, collecting the largest purse in the sport at the time. Today, King still drives the team-tennis movement where men and women play and compete together as equals. *Gloria Steinem,* acclaimed feminist, professional, and single working mother, founded *Ms.* magazine and worked to shed candid light on women's very real work and life issues. Steinem also fought to protect battered women and against sexual harassment. She was instrumental in the passing of the Equal Rights Amendment in 1978. When interviewed recently on the state of the feminist movement today, Steinem had this to say: "The feminist revolution is the longest revolution in history. I'm not sure we're half-way through this process. Maybe only a third. That's why I say to take it in 100-year stretches. Movements have to last at least a century to be fully absorbed and normalized in culture."[25]

Princess Diana moved masses with her uniquely melded activism and vulnerability. Named the "people's princess" for her ordinary appeal, Diana sought to leverage her position for the advancement of social causes. Diana was revered for interacting publically with transparency and genuineness. Her activism extended beyond global matters to something very personal to her—her marriage. Princess Diana spoke out openly about her husband's infidelity. Heir apparent to the throne or not, Diana held Prince Charles to the same standards she believed any spouse should follow regardless of the opposition she faced from other members of the royal family.

Georgia O'Keeffe, an independent and gifted artist, lived by no one's social rules but her own. O'Keeffe realized her creative vision in works of art that transcended those of her time. She was the first acclaimed female artist and rose to further recognition as a top American modern artist overall in a field still male ruled today. In addition to her creative brilliance, what marks O'Keeffe's cultural contribution as astonishing is the open expression it inspires in all of us. One need only view an O'Keeffe painting to be gently, completely, and powerfully freed in mind and spirit. Hers is a truly feminine force. O'Keefe's independence is noteworthy as she was in a committed, loving relationship and was so from a lifestyle perspective that a woman could be both a committed partner and an independent, aspiring woman. Throughout O'Keeffe's marriage to noted photographer Alfred Stieglitz she continued to live her own life and be her own person back when it was difficult enough for a woman to choose career over marriage and family.[26]

This initial recap of inspirational women concludes with perhaps the ultimate maternal figure, *Mother Theresa*. Mother Theresa founded the Missionaries of Charity and for almost 50 years led efforts to assist those deeply deprived. Mother Theresa was awarded the Noble Prize for Peace in 1979 for her complete and selfless devotion to those in need. All of these inspirational women's contributions are marked by the feminine brand of *directive force*—formidable closure-seeking attention to the task at hand and yet another key feminine leadership trait.

WHERE DO WE GO FROM HERE?

Considering the recounted stories of each of these astonishing women, it is hard to imagine why we still have so far to go to reach equality for women. Yet that is the harsh truth. There are countless additional inspirational stories to be told, and still leadership has not opened its doors to the potent feminine brand. Perhaps some recent data will help to convince us of both the validity of this complaint and the conundrum at hand. In a 2011 study by Jack Zenger and Joseph Folkman, 7,280 leaders were studied. Using ratings from peers, bosses, and direct reports, respondents were asked to rate each leader's effectiveness overall and to rate them further on 16 specific competencies found to be critical to successful leadership. Women leaders rated higher in the more expected feminine traits such as developing others, building relationships, acting with integrity, and pursuing self-development. What was also found might surprise some. Women scored higher across the board as better overall leaders. The two traits that women scored highest on were taking initiative and driving for results, which, according to Zenger and Folkman, are seen more typically as male strong suits. Zenger and Folkman then queried women anecdotally for an explanation of the results and found that some women continue to work harder to drive for results because they believe they need to continue to prove themselves—in essence, to be better than men in order to get the same recognition.[27]

When I read Zenger and Folkman's findings, my conclusions were a bit different. We are all pushed to work harder today. The demands on everyone are higher. The fact that women are outscoring men today on the more feminine leadership traits is less germane than the fact that feminine traits continue to come through as crucial leadership drivers. The fact that women also scored higher overall, and in particular on traits thought previously to reflect more male-based inclinations such as getting the job done, is no surprise at all. This data point validates the activities that women have been engaged in in order to make their way; managing multifarious role demands and fighting for parity are propellants of leadership. Put another way, over time, our collective life experiences have provided a formidable leadership training program and, therefore, netted us an exceptional leadership résumé.

So where do we go from here? We realize that the basic sociocultural foundations that women lead through are in fact potent and warrant incorporation. We move to create the new normal by giving women greater leadership voice and opportunity. Most importantly, senior leaders and human resources structures must formally reorganize to position themselves so that they can substantively champion, drive, and support the incorporation of feminine models into existing operating cultures.

IDEA-BASED LEADERSHIP: THE NEW NORMAL

What you are about to discover is a leadership model that calls out the four key traits for success born from the true *complete* feminine perspective. Those traits include *intuitive* orientation, *directive* force, *empowering* intent, and *assimilative* nature. The acronym for the traits, then, is IDEA, and the model is called IDEA-based leadership. IDEA-based leadership is a simple path for leaders to follow and encompass. It begins with your ability as a leader to gain both insight and foresight as you set out to understand current realities, create a vision, and determine appropriate directions. The caveat here is that you do so from the mindset of a loyal steward. You are collectively rather than self-aimed. Next you move to accomplish what you need to. You are the consummate planner, tactician, and executor. As you do so, you involve those around you in a manner that builds momentum and productivity—you empower. Lastly, you integrate everything as an evolved construct. You take all that was and combine it with the newly realized, assimilating it into an advanced state.

The IDEA-based model emanates from female sociocultural mores. As such, women are more prone to act from this model, but many men naturally incorporate some or all of these constructs into their ways of leading. The book does not attempt to suggest that *all* women or *all* men act one way or another. Men and women alike can and have assumed the IDEA-based traits. The book does, however, strongly put forth that this feminine-born model is in many regards more likely to be realized when women are in the highest positions of authority. Men and women alike who act from IDEA-based traits in traditionally male-led arenas come up against ingrained resistance that undermines the evolved leader's realized impact.

Over the next four chapters you will learn more about each of the four IDEA traits. You will also learn of prominent leaders of the present day who serve as exemplars. The final chapter presents a synthesis of the four key traits along with considerations for greater overall leadership integration and success. Tools are offered along the way to help you apply the model to your current leadership challenges. Finally, strategies are suggested for making your organizations, work groups, and teams more gender integrated and free of constricting and impeding biases and pitfalls.

CHAPTER 2

An Intuitive Orientation

Intuition is a spiritual faculty and does not explain, but simply points the way.
—Florence Scovel Shinn[1]

WOMEN'S INTUITION

Consider the following excerpt from Dyhan Giten, an internationally recognized teacher and advisor to organizations. Giten's work centers around developing greater awareness in organizations and on the power of intuition. Giten relays, "To see life from the perspective of intuition is to have vision. To see life from the perspective of intuition is like looking at life from the summit of the mountain, whereas seeing life only from the perspective of intellect is like looking at life from the foot of the mountain. Through learning to listen to our intuition, we learn to be in contact with the Whole."[2]

If your preference is for intuitive thought, you see patterns, trends, and themes. You see future possibilities. Most importantly, you have a more complete and unobstructed view. Accomplished strategic thinkers apply their intuition at the broadest possible levels, to the big picture, globally and holistically. They take their vision—that which could be—and craft overarching approaches to get there while paying full attention to the all-inclusive context. Intuition is primal to sound leadership, and women are socialized to access the intuitive portion of their brains. Why is this so? Their historic social roles have compelled them to do so. With a fundamental focus on caretaking and nurturing, women have been positioned to listen and to observe, to be on the alert, and to watch for signs of how those in their care are doing. Such a vantage point predisposes one to right-brain reflection, to consideration of possibilities, and to thinking in terms of precautions and unknowns. A woman's world is in this sense grounded in "what could be." Women are engaged in a continuous quest for meaning and for what might occur.

Men on the other hand, are historically inclined to assert their position and to surge ahead based on those assertions. In this sense, men have been socialized to left-brain tangibles. They are drawn to the world of "what is" in order to perform and accomplish. As a case in point, I was recently with clients at an off-site planning session. They were discussing top issues and ways to address problems. To a person, the men in the group went directly to options for faster turnaround in the profit numbers while the women were raising points that, in their minds, explored what seemed to be standing in the way of progress. The men saw the women's direction as unnecessary. The senior leader referred to it as "unnecessary drama," something we couldn't know for sure and therefore shouldn't waste time on. If you think, however, about the nature of our issues today, many of the matters we grapple with are not clear-cut. We are frequently confronted with ambiguity and with unknowns. Now more than ever, we are expected to make leaps and to infer, to play out numerous scenarios, and to think of potential threats and ramifications. As we attempt to solve problems of all sorts, being able to consider both current (quantifiable) realities and that which is implicit or conceivable enables a more complete examination. Intuitive data becomes crucial in our decision making. Exploring possible causal scenarios is not unnecessary drama. It is a necessary part of our thinking process.

The term *women's intuition* came to pass to position sensing as a feminine inclination. While this has long been disputed as fact or fiction, women do seem to exercise their intuition more than men. The consideration here is not about who is better at one thing or another. Women have come to see the value of intuitive thought. They see its broadest applicability. They have direct and repeated experience with it. It serves them well and directs them. For women, intuition is an internalized and proven essential skill.

My husband is actually quite intuitive when he wants to be. While I spend more time thinking in "what ifs" than he does, he is spot-on in his insights. He had a long and successful leadership career driving for results, but his ability to preface that drive with *intuitive* vision is what set him apart. It was his key differentiator. He was poised to read between the lines, leveraging perspicacious thinking to his leadership advantage. The viewpoint conveyed here then is that women are more prone to intuitive thought not because they have greater capability but because the nature of their experiences—their sociocultural roles—have inspired it. We all have within us the right-brain potential for intuitive thought. We need only believe in it and practice it. Men and women alike who start their leadership process with intuitions have a distinct edge. Rather than cementing yourself exclusively in the present, open up your mind to other possibilities, to meaning, and to what trends and patterns tell us.

INTUITION DECONSTRUCTED

So what precisely is intuition as it relates to how we need to lead today? The most basic definitions of intuition would describe it as something you know instinctively. Intuition might be described as a keen awareness gleaned from sensory cues and inferences. More specifically with respect to our brain and thinking, intuition is a trait more associated with the right brain rather than the left. The left brain controls sequential and linear thought. The right brain controls emotional and imaginative thinking. The left brain is where our analytical abilities come from. As such, it helps us see things as they are. The left brain reasons from parts to the whole. The right brain, on the other hand, is holistic; it reasons from the whole to parts. The right brain is reflective and helps us see things for how they could be. Women's historic socialization and more recent multifarious role demands encourage both a right- and left-brain workout, whereas men are more prone to leverage the left brain to a greater extent. When considering intuition as a right-brain propensity, women have certainly been disposed to engage in "what if" thinking more routinely.[3]

In both our current personal and professional arenas, right-brain intuitive thought is needed to more succinctly gauge what is possible given the constricted platforms we are operating from. We are under time, money, and people constraints in virtually all aspects of our lives; we are expected to do more with less. In spite of these limitations, we are still held to higher outputs. Whether tending to our families or refining a market position at work, we need to read the tea leaves ever so carefully in order to get it right. We don't always have all the information. Several important questions may remain unanswered, and still we have to make a decision. We have to be able to take our best calculated guess. When is the right time personally, for example, to place an aging parent in assisted living, and, more importantly, how should we go about it? How should we communicate this to our loved one? Certainly, straightforward data from the doctor comes directly into play, yet there is far more to consider. We need to *feel* our way through extraneous factors in order to properly address this complex existential matter in the most positive way possible. That can only be accomplished when the intuitive orientation melds with the factual.

In the past, we had more buffer room. If we were making determinations on the work front about new hires or promoting from within, we had room for a margin of error. There was always somewhere we could move the person we promoted if it didn't work out. Not so today. If we make a move and it doesn't work out, it will likely mean there is nowhere else for that individual to go. We could be left having to terminate the person and deal with an even greater resource gap from the failure of the move, the time wasted, and the resulting fallout. Decisions of this nature need to be made from Giten's right-brain, holistic view—from the top of the mountain. Tapping into our left brain alone will leave us coming up short time and time again. Leaders need to act from a broader range of skills, the first of which is their emotional intelligence, in order to engage and hone precious intuitive thinking.

Emotional intelligence is a concept created by Daniel Goleman. Emotional intelligence showcases the importance of self- and other-awareness as key factors in our effectiveness and success. Goleman's groundbreaking theory teaches us how such awareness is, in Goleman's view, more important than IQ in determining how successful we will be. Emotional intelligence can be summarized as having four distinct aspects. The first component is having as complete knowledge of our self as possible. More specifically, self-awareness begins with knowing our own personality style, inclinations, and tendencies. As you drill deeper, self-awareness involves knowing our cultural orientations and how those perspectives shape our values, reactions, and behaviors. Get deeper still, and we would want to understand when we are at our best, how stress affects us, why we are drawn to certain people and situations more than others, and how we are perceived by others.

The second aspect of emotional intelligence is awareness of others. Other-awareness would be having that same information about the people who matter to us, those we relate to and interact with regularly. Ultimately, one would want one's other-awareness to develop to the point that we would be able to read anyone we encounter quickly and with accuracy.

The two final components of emotional intelligence involve what we do with our self- and other-awareness—how we manage ourselves and our interactions. Self- and other-management includes how we shape our communication to a particular audience, how to know what to do and say in sensitive conversations, and how to best develop others. Self- and other-management is the crucial differentiator to the Goleman brand of leadership and life success.[4] Think of it as a piece of exercise equipment you set out to purchase in order to become more physically fit. You first research and select the make and model that is right for you. Next you get the equipment home and assemble it. Think of this phase of your fitness program as Goleman's self- and other-awareness. The equipment does not deliver any benefit, though, until you actually work out on it. Self- and other-management is analogous to your actual fitness workout. Learning how to react to the cognizance you have acquired is what gives you leadership strength, impact, and resilience—leadership fitness, if you will.

TUNING IN: THE POWER OF AWARENESS

For many years I taught a course in group dynamics. The course covered a range of topics with self-, other-, and context-awareness as foundational. According to leading self-awareness theorists Joseph Luft and Harry Ingham, when you think of awareness, there are four levels to consider: *open*—that which is readily apparent (what is out in the open, observable, and measurable); *blind*—that which is not yet acknowledged (there, but masked by our blind spots); *hidden*—that which is willfully concealed (purposely secreted); and *unknown*—that which has yet to be discovered.[5] For our purposes we will focus on the first three. *Open awareness* concerns what most of us can observe and understand. It is tangible. Included in this category would be things that are factual in nature, such as how long someone has worked in his or her present job or a company's total sales for last year. The second aspect of awareness, blind awareness, consists of things about us or our circumstance that are true and accurate but that we refuse to see. We are told something, but we can't imagine it to be so, or, worse yet, we deny its validity because we can't accept it. Such blind spots are of serious concern because they can potentially leave us most vulnerable.

Think of Pearl Harbor, the *Challenger* disaster, and the events of 9/11. Each of these tragedies was to some extent enabled through facts we had some awareness of but could not fathom, and therefore we didn't take interventional action. Prior to the attacks on Pearl Harbor we had information that the Japanese were going to attack. We couldn't imagine that they would do so. Individuals working on the space shuttle prior to the *Challenger* disaster knew of certain technical flaws, yet it was incomprehensible that the result would be so disastrous. We had knowledge of terrorists plotting to use commercial aircraft as weapons yet couldn't believe such a plot could come to fruition. I am sure you can think of examples in your own personal or professional lives where blind spots set you back. They are destructive and compromising.

Personal blind spots place us at a disadvantage because others see things about us that we don't. Perceptions are formed that we are unaware of. We are, in essence, operating from a compromised reality. Blind spots can be enabled through our biases; we hold a particular belief that prevents us from seeing or accepting something about us. For example, if I believed that people are unquestionably trustworthy, I would not see that others saw me as gullible. Blind spots can also be caused by denial. We refuse to accept that our marriage is failing, and therefore don't take seriously our spouse's insistence to work on our problems. Blind spots can also be caused by our own drive. If leaders are compelled to a certain goal by a certain date, they are less likely to hear or accept feedback about shortcomings; they are too focused on the goal to see the minefield they are walking into. Sound intuitive leaders see blind spots for the serious threats they pose and work continuously to uncover and address them. Blind spots are natural and dynamic; we will always have them, and they are ever-changing. The emotionally intelligent leader is engaged in an unremitting process of self-discovery in order to be alerted to and address them.

The final type of awareness for consideration, *hidden awareness,* or that which is willfully concealed, can be equally harmful to those who are not "in the know." When someone is acting with hidden agendas, you can be as equally blind-sided as you could be through your own denial. Some of us purposely and appropriately conceal things because they are private—only to be shared with those we are close to. Sometimes we hide things for our own protection; however, sometimes things are concealed to give one person a decided advantage. This is what is meant by a hidden agenda. If we think about the global banking crisis that brought the world to the brink of financial ruin, we can see the most nefarious reaches of hidden awareness. This fiasco came, no doubt, from multiple levels of leaders' blind spots as well as willful hidden agendas. Hidden agendas are self-serving and can place others at serious risk.

Hidden agendas come in all shapes and sizes from the tiniest of omissions to complex plotting. Those who engage in hidden agendas are by nature highly political—they are constantly maneuvering in order to get ahead. Sound intuition will cue you into this political type. Their behavior is considered self-centered in nature. In many instances, their integrity can be questionable. Organizational-savvy authors Rick Brandon and Marty Seldman describe the overly political as those who "start out with a strong set of principles, but power, ambition, pressure or greed seduce them into compromising their value system."[6] You can see how being aware of those who function from an overly political perspective, who use hidden awareness to their advantage, is crucial to your protection and preservation. Sound intuition can also help you become rightly savvy, what Brandon and Seldman refer to as having impact with integrity. Your shrewd awareness helps you properly negotiate political landscapes, lobby effectively, and promote yourself in a genuine manner.

Awareness is the foundation of Gestalt psychology, a perspective based on the concept that the Gestalt (the German word for "whole") is greater than the sum of its parts. Gestalt psychology emphasizes three points: an accurate view of reality, personal responsibility, and the ability to govern outcomes. This perspective further emphasizes attention to the present, making the present what we want and need it to be. An adequate present is obtained through understanding past experiences and implications, by bringing unpleasant re-collections to closure, and by being realistic in our hopes for the future.[7] There are direct tie-ins from the Gestalt perspective to the place of awareness in intuitive leadership. The Gestalt perspective of the whole being greater than the sum of its parts is the essence of being strategic. To gain a better appreciation of the whole and hence to gain better strategic appreciation is, in Gestalt terms, accomplished through one's awareness of present realities and the insights one gleans therein. Women are more inclined to seek out information about themselves, others, and their surroundings. They have a curiosity and a compulsion to know in Gestalt terms. Their intuitive sense gives them an appreciation of the interconnectedness of people, places, and events, and in that sense their intuitive side is fed and honed.

To have greater intuitive leadership skill, then, you need to be fundamentally adept at all levels of awareness—*open*, *blind*, and *hidden*. Additionally, those levels of awareness need to be applied to three dimensions of your life: to how you see yourself, to your understanding of others, and to your current life contexts. Had we been able to think in terms of other- and context-awareness, for example, when the intelligence came in regarding Pearl Harbor, the *Challenger* disaster, or the 9/11 attacks, we may have been able to see the inconceivable as possible. We use the phrase, "hindsight is twenty-twenty" to mean that once something actually occurs, it is clearer to us how it could have happened in the first place. That view discounts the advantage we could have with greater awareness. While we will never be able to accurately predict everything, we can surely get closer by developing better awareness. If you are instead, however, disposed to think from insular perspectives and contexts, you increase the chances that you will tune out diverse realities. As such, you leave yourself operating at a disadvantage. Stifled awareness, whether about you, about others in your realm, or about the present context can render even the brightest and most capable of leaders oblivious to certain truths. Incomplete awareness on any level is a leader's greatest threat, while keen awareness is a leader's ultimate asset.

FEEDBACK: THE KEY TO AWARENESS

Intuition is fostered as we gain greater overall awareness. Intuition is also cultivated through the development of empathy because empathy gives us a window into the perceptions of others. Attending to feedback is a primary means of facilitating awareness and therefore of developing intuition. Attending to feedback is also fundamental to the development of empathy. As an intuitive leader, you need a working knowledge of how others see you, your team, and your business contributions. As an individual, your relational success comes from similar understandings. You need to know how you are perceived by those most important to you, what your interpersonal strong suits are, and how your vulnerabilities are triggered and expressed. Once you identify what impressions others have of you, you can evaluate which are accurate, where your blind spots may be, and where misperceptions may exist. You are then in a position to address incongruities. You are, in effect, in better control of your destiny.

Feedback can come to us from multiple sources. It can be attained directly as something written about you formally in a performance evaluation or informally in a letter, email, or text. It can come from various assessment tools that target broad or specific aspects of your personality, values, style, or leadership. It can be told to you by a trusted family member, friend, or colleague. You can provide yourself with feedback by better attuning to and understanding your behavior as well as the behavior of others. Especially crucial is the attention you give to the nonverbal aspects of communication: someone's facial expressions, tone of voice, eye contact, body language, and the like. Nonverbal communication is said to comprise upwards of 85 percent of our communication. It provides a wealth of information that appreciably bolsters one's awareness. Feedback can come from the more intuitive "reading between the lines," or paying attention to what's not said or to what is inferred. As such, feedback is a self- and other-awareness tool.

Important to note is the fact that feedback should not always be taken literally. It may be inaccurate or not mean what is stated, but it always does mean something. It takes an investigative mind to get to its true meaning. Whenever I think of feedback, I am reminded of the time when I was teaching and a student wrote something on an evaluation that shocked me. I was a relatively new professor. I loved teaching and thought I had solid relationships with my students. At the end of every semester, we were handed the famed green envelope. In it were our course evaluations—hundreds of pages of comments and ratings. It was a lot of material to sort through. On this particular day, I was relaxing into the semester's end, quietly tucked away in my office reading through what students had written. There were many validating statements. As I got further down into the pile, there it was. A student had written, "She was the biggest disappointment in my life." "Well, that wasn't very nice," I thought. I was actually stunned. I kept on reading, page by page, and most of the other evaluations were fine. There were a few mild suggestions and criticisms, but nothing like this.

Now I began to get annoyed: "Is this person serious, seeing me as the biggest disappointment?" I took a deep breath and began to think. I decided that, logically speaking, because I didn't recall any incidents during the semester that warranted such a comment, something else was at work here. But what could it be? To make a very long story short, I eventually got to the point of acceptance that I had done something that required further scrutiny. Such is the process with feedback, especially difficult feedback. It can be hard to digest at first. When it is extreme or off-putting, there is a tendency to dismiss it altogether. I examined what this particular student said next to the other less harsh but still critical statements.

I talked things over with a colleague who knew me well. The conclusion reached was that my interpersonal style may be confusing to some. Especially for the student in question, my style apparently sent the wrong signals. The following semester I began to adjust my manner. I was also more explicit about my nature and my intent. From that point on, the negative comments went away and stayed away. I was able to have close relationships with my students but added an element of communication clarity that seemed to help them know where I was coming from. As I continued on in my career and issues arose, I applied the same technology for processing feedback, with continued positive results. I looked openly at what was said. I noted converging lines of evidence—what may have been said more than once or by different individuals. I sought out a trusted colleague to discuss the matter with. I did all of this in order to put the pieces together as best as I could. Feedback became my trusted ally. It gave me an edge, a development process I could count on.

There are two morals to this story. The first is that feedback cannot always be taken literally; meanings must be interpreted or inferred from what is actually reported, written, or said. The second is that knee-jerk reactions to tough feedback are normal. You must give yourself the time to move through them in order to arrive at a place of understanding. What you do from there will make all the difference. The thing to remember is that if you don't reconcile the feedback, the negative information about you will still be out there. As long as you ignore it or cannot accept what you come to know, valuable information about you will be in others' hands. Think of it this way. When you see yourself on a video or hear yourself on tape, you almost always notice things that you didn't realize before, or you may find it hard to believe that you sound, look, or come across in certain ways. Without the vantage point of looking directly at yourself, you can be *blind* to certain aspects of your manner. Others have the opportunity for direct observation all the time. Fortunately for us, most often others are preoccupied with their own issues and are not attending exclusively to us. When we are under their direct scrutiny, however, they can and do still glean valuable information about us. Others also form opinions readily and sometimes without basis. The key is to be privy to that information. Feedback is the way to do that.

Debborah Himsel, an author and leadership expert, wrote a book several years back about an unorthodox leader. That leader is a fictitious former television character, mafia leader Tony Soprano. In a provocative and humorous analysis, Soprano's leadership qualities were examined. One quality was his ability to deal with feedback. Tony actually received high feedback marks for his willingness to ask for it directly—in Himsel's words, "to his face." This is not such an easy thing to do. Himsel has this to say about feedback:

- Feedback is not something to fear; reframe it from potentially hurtful to necessary.
- If you don't like it, you do have the option of disagreeing with it.
- People's intentions are usually good, meaning they are trying to protect or help you.
- Be proactive in going after the feedback rather than being a source of gossip.
- Don't personalize feedback. In Himsel's words, "don't shoot the messenger." Maintain your composure and listen.[8]

This is sound advice from Himsel, especially the part about maintaining your cool. Feedback cuts directly to our self-esteem. The question you have to ask yourself is: Do I want to be told I am great, or do I want to know how to become great? Consider adopting a process for making feedback a regular part of your life. It needs to become second nature to you for all the good it has to offer. Lastly, when reflecting on the feedback you receive, look for true meaning. Get below the surface to the heart of messages.

In closing this section on awareness, think of the added potency you will have as a leader by making use of all of the information truly at your disposal, not just the information that supports your current thinking or desired direction. Through making use of feedback we attain greater, multitiered awareness. Great awareness on all fronts gives us more places to connect the dots and to hone our intuitive acumen. Intuition gives us a decided leadership advantage. So next time you hear the phrase *women's intuition* being applied to someone, don't be so quick to dismiss what she is thinking as trite or unfounded. It's likely not "drama." It is, rather, valuable information. She has probably had a lifetime of *tuning in* to ground her view.

If anything, women are inclined to be overly disposed to awareness. A case in point comes from the perspective of Google's senior vice president of people operations, Lazzlo Bock. Mr. Bock was interviewed by Dennis Berman at the Women in the Economy Conference in May 2012. Bock described Google as highly team oriented and stated that the company runs better with more women. Bock further described an interesting dynamic in Google's promotion process. Anyone can nominate themselves at any time for a promotion at Google. Bock noted behavioral differences that are awareness-based between men and women with respect to this process. Men at Google are promoted a certain percentage of the time that they nominate themselves, whereas women are always promoted. Bock attributes this statistical difference to awareness. He described men as less self-aware than women. Bock further noted that men think more of their ability than may be reality, whereas women scrutinize themselves more and are probably in fact ready sooner than they think to be promoted. Bock stated that the more complex context women operate from may cause them to wait beyond their readiness point to apply.[9] My intuition tells me that women are waiting until they are certain they have all bases covered because they are considering more than their work capability in determining their readiness for a bigger role.

In an article entitled "Leadership: Qualities That Distinguish Women," Herbert Greenberg and Patrick Sweeney describe the results of a study that pointed to several personality and motivational strengths that women possess that the authors say are "more conducive to today's workplace." With respect to the topics of intuition and awareness, Greenberg and Sweeney note that the particular interpersonal skills that women leaders leverage enable them to "read situations accurately and take in information from all sides." The authors specifically view this preference that the women leaders they studied have for "taking it all in" as enhancing not only the leaders' decision-making abilities but their persuasive abilities as well. Greenberg and Sweeney believe this is the case because women truly want to understand others' perspectives and, because of that, they are more readily able to influence. Those around them feel heard and valued and are therefore more likely to listen in turn.

Several key examples of executive-level leaders using this style were provided, including one of a chief financial officer (CFO) who stated that when she is trying to convince someone, she spends more time understanding their perspective than driving hers. Greenberg and Sweeney referred to this as an engaging style of persuasion. The second intuition-based skill noted in the Greenberg/Sweeney report was women's willingness to take risks. This finding was reported as unexpected because we typically see men as more risk-taking than women. Specifically, the study noted that women were less interested in what "has been" and more interested in working toward what "can be." Women were found to possess the willingness to head into the unknown, to forge a path forward, and to learn from mistakes.[10] The fact that women were found to function well in unchartered waters is no surprise if we factor in their awareness-fueled intuitive sense.

INTUITION-BUILDING 101

Intuition can be cultivated by involving yourself in a number of activities. Three specific development tools are offered here. They are quieting your mind, active listening, and formal reflection. Each development tool draws upon right- rather than left-brain strengths. If you think about how much of our day-to-day existence pulls us to our left brain—to the tangible, the closure-seeking, and the immediate—it is clear that by engaging in activities that stimulate right-brain thinking we encourage intuitive thought, and more importantly, we better leverage our full brain in the dual manner for which it was intended. We tend to typically act from constricted preferences. Our brains, however, are set up for decidedly more. You may have heard it said that we only use a small part of our brains. For most of us, this is certainly true. Expressions like "we are creatures of habit" and "great minds think alike" illustrate our tendencies toward what is known and familiar. The expression "opposites attract" refers to an emotional pull, an excitement we feel when we are in the company of someone or something different. All too often, though, our excitement turns sour. While we gravitate toward the novel, we are socialized to feel most secure with what we already know. We sometimes refer to the angst experienced as "stepping out of our comfort zone," another indicator of how we unwittingly thwart our brain's diverse potential. By focusing on *alter-brain behaviors*[11] (right- rather than left-brain inclinations), our brain's natural power can be released.

Quieting your mind is the first right-brain activity you can engage in to build intuitive thought. Quieting your mind is foundational to the intuitive process. It involves providing a break from your forward movement, that constant expectation for you to accomplish and advance. It literally involves stopping yourself, freezing time if you will, so that your mind can clear itself from the incessant surge of mental and emotional activity. Quieting your mind is achieved by allowing yourself short periods of time each day where you stop everything and simply sit at peace and in silence. This may sound a bit odd as many of us are used to operating at lightning speed all day long. When we do take the time to relax, we are usually still in receiver mode, whether it be time spent mindlessly surfing the Internet, watching television, listening to music, or engaged in conversation. What is instead suggested here is to truly give your mind a break.

Quieting your mind is thus accomplished by sitting or lying down in a comfortable space. If possible, situating yourself somewhere outdoors or nature-based is optimal. Close your eyes and begin to clear your mind. As thoughts of your day and life intrude, focus on your breathing and just be still. Try to do this for 5 to 10 minutes a day. You will be amazed at the result. Your mind will open up, and aspects of your deeper right-brain thoughts will surface. This activity is easier said than done. It takes practice to resist distractions and to experience silence. We are not used to it. For many of us, the only time we experience silence is when we are asleep. Still, though, as you try this activity over and over again, you will experience a comforting form of relaxation and control over an otherwise pressured existence. Think of it as a maintenance activity, like when we defragment our computers. We are optimizing space so that the computer runs better. Quieting your mind is similar. It releases the backlog of mental and emotional clutter so that we can think more clearly.[12]

The second intuition-building activity is *active listening*. Active listening has three components: attending, paraphrasing, and validating. You begin by cuing in to what the other person is saying, not just to the words or the topic but to the nature of what he or she is saying—what meaning it has. Next you paraphrase back what you heard. You don't parrot the other's words, but in your own words capture the essence of what he or she is conveying. The final aspect of active listening is validation. This is a gut-check of sorts, giving the other person a chance to tell you how close or far off you are and to provide more information if necessary.

Active listening enables an other- rather than self-focused dialogue. As such it helps you to develop empathy. You will tune in to greater information, to new perspectives, and to the more right-brain nonverbal cues. As you practice active listening and develop greater empathy, you will become more naturally intuitive. The most difficult part in mastering empathy, for many, is in slowing your forward momentum. To take the time to shift our focus from our sales pitch to understanding where someone else is coming from can seem like we are backtracking or losing ground. In fact, the opposite is the case. Taking the time to be more empathic gives you valuable information and perspectives into those around you that can better inform you, broaden your view, and at times keep you from being blind-sided while at the same time building intuitive power.[13]

The final intuitive activity is *formal reflection*. Afford yourself time each day to think about what you have done or are setting out to do. Rather than springing into action, step back and reflect. Look for the meaning of what you are trying to accomplish or for the meaning in what has already occurred. The method suggested here draws on the principles of qualitative research, specifically on the research method of phenomenology. Phenomenology is the study of an experience. It involves reflection on our views, our perspectives, and our interpretations. It helps us to become aware of and to understand the nature and meaning of what we are involved in.[14] Reflecting involves setting aside time to think. It is a more passive than an active endeavor. One may typically confuse problem-solving pursuits with reflection. When you problem solve, you go after an issue in an active and often structured manner. You get up in from of a white board and begin diagramming or listing. You look at data, and you may even dialogue with others.

The reflection described here more refers to an open-ended pondering, something done alone where you allow your mind the freedom to wander and to consider. You would begin with a central question and perhaps two to four subquestions. Next, sit quietly and consider the nature of all that is involved in your central query. When capturing your thoughts, do so through unstructured phrases and simple drawings, symbols to represent what you have discovered. Such amorphous thoughts and images pull from your right (intuitive) brain, whereas organized writing such as lists and outlines are a left-brain process. The more time you spend prompting right-brain activity, and specifically right-brain activity that asks your brain to configure on its own, the more intuitive you will become.

You can see by the activities suggested to encourage intuitive thought that intuition requires room to surface; it is less likely to be accessed when we are moving tenaciously forward, and it needs actual thought space in order to appear. Second, the more facile we are at all forms of listening, but especially at active listening (reading people and situations), the more intuitive we stand to be. This very special form of listening is accomplished through the kindling of our empathic acumen. Lastly, we need to be able to consider and to reflect on what occurs regularly and fluidly so that we become more phenomenological in our orientation; we are tuned in to the nature of our experiences. With these three simply accessed tools, greater intuitive thought is not only possible but becomes a more internalized part of our thinking.

INTUITIVE EXEMPLARS

Christine Lagarde

Christine Lagarde was the first woman chairman of the prestigious Chicago-based law firm Baker & McKenzie, the first female finance minister of France, and now the first female head of the International Monetary Fund (IMF), replacing ousted countryman Dominique Strauss-Kahn. A woman now sits at the head of the world's most powerful financial institution, in a field clearly and unequivocally dominated by men. Lagarde has many leadership strong suits. Those strong suits are grounded in her intuitive wisdom. She is known for her competence, calm, and her candor, all necessary traits to possess given her current role. She demonstrates full-brain engagement, blending quintessential right-brain vision with flawless left-brain execution.

When asked in December 2011 by Gillian Tett, the U.S. managing editor of *Financial Times*, if the 2008 global financial crisis would have been different with more women in finance, she replied, "My intuition tells me it might have been." What an interesting choice of words. Lagarde went on to jokingly ask us to think about how things would have been different if there were Lehman sisters instead of brothers and if we had founding mothers instead of fathers, referring in this particular case to the lack of feminine influence in the world of money, banking, finance, and governance.

Lagarde came from humble beginnings, the oldest of four and the only female sibling. Her parents stressed scholarship, her father being a university professor. It is reported that her parents' rearing tenor was both strict and loving. The nature of her schooling and experiences socialized her to be as formidable as she is collaborative. Her life precipitously changed, however, when her father died at an early age. Lagarde was 16 at the time, and her mother carried on in inspirational fashion. Lagarde's maternal grandmother was recalled as a strong role model as well. She was a nurse during the First World War and a remarkably independent woman.[15] Lagarde experienced much duality in her upbringing and experiences. This confluence nurtured her brain to develop in an optimally complex fashion that is grounded in reflection. French culture is after all steeped in the contemplative. As René Descartes so aptly put it, "I think, therefore I am," noting how thought is primal to existence.

Lagarde spent much of her adult life studying and working in the United States or in American-influenced circumstances. The American cultural influence is based more on doing; it is a culture of action. Lagarde's intuitive roots begat artful implementation. In November 2011, *60 Minutes* correspondent Lara Logan also interviewed Lagarde following her appointment as IMF head. Logan's interview was moving in that we were able to observe Lagarde's full range of leadership aptitude in action. One question in particular stood out that is germane here. Lagarde was speaking about assuming her role at a time of potentially catastrophic fallout from the then-current European debt crisis. Logan asked Lagarde what the worst-case scenario might be. Without pause, Lagarde stated the following likelihoods: high unemployment, stalled growth, social unrest, and financial markets in disarray.[16] While there is historical data to inform her response, an equal degree of conjecture is required. Lagarde's intuitive sense makes her fundamentally superior at what she does. It provides the basis for the negotiating skills she draws on to influence heads of state and ingrained cultural perspectives. It tells her when the IMF should operate in authoritative fashion and when it should instill empowerment in governments and institutions. As such, Lagarde is noted here as an intuitive exemplar *par excellence*.

Julie Aigner-Clark

From *Forbes*'s Most Powerful Woman of 2011 and IMF head we move to a stay-at-home mom and former teacher, Julie Aigner-Clark. Aigner-Clark had an intuitive inspiration as she was raising her young daughters. That inspiration birthed Baby Einstein, a line of multimedia products for young children that brought in Aigner-Clark's appreciation for art and humanity. The products were designed in such a way that parents could meaningfully interact with their children. Baby Einstein products continue to employ novel aspects of nature, art, music, and animals to facilitate an exciting parent-child discovery of the world.

Production and sales began from Aigner-Clark's home in 1996. It is reported that she drew her logo while sitting at her kitchen table and the first video was produced in their basement using a home computer. Aigner-Clark and her husband's initial investment was $18,000. The company quickly grew to a multimillion-dollar franchise selling its product in over 30 countries. It is now estimated that the brand is valued in the hundreds of millions of dollars, and the Baby Einstein line is listed as the top-selling brand in its class. Aigner-Clark was named Entrepreneur of the Year and has won numerous other product honors.[17] In order for Baby Einstein to be the success it is, Aigner-Clark had to possess the ability to see into the future and know that what she envisioned could actually work. She had to position the product so that it would be well received in the broadest possible sense. That takes honed intuitive skill.

The New Power Girls

Entrepreneurship, like other aspects of business, has historically been male dominated, but women are quickly and furiously infiltrating this niche. When initially researching famous entrepreneurs, renowned female icons Oprah Winfrey and Estée Lauder were listed alongside a host of male counterparts such as Henry Ford, Bill Gates, and Ray Crock, to name a few. When searching famous female entrepreneurs, what was interesting was the compelling nature of the women's contributions. For example, Mary Kay Ash is the founder of Mary Kay Cosmetics. Not only did Ash build a successful enterprise, but the business model and channel distribution she chose enabled several hundred thousand women to become business owners themselves as independent sales representatives for the Mary Kay product lines. Also in the cosmetics industry, Anita Roddick founded The Body Shop. Roddick was both a businesswoman and activist. She pioneered the production of natural cosmetics and worked in tandem to promote civil and human rights. A primary thrust in her company's marketing campaigns was to promote esteem-building in women, working to dispel the myths about what is referred to as "magazine model beauty." Additionally, Roddick fought tirelessly against the inhumane treatment of animals in the testing of cosmetic products.[18]

Madame C. J. Walker is noted as the first female African American millionaire. Walker's enterprise was also credited for employing thousands of people in a business endeavor known for its exceptionally high-integrity-based operating practices. Walker built her empire in 15 years selling hair care and beauty products to African American women in the early 1900s. Walker's motivation came from a personal experience with a scalp disorder. She created numerous home remedies with astonishing results. Her products and methods took off. She attributes her success to tenacity and ferocity in her work effort coupled with attention to ethics in how she developed her products and services and treated those who worked for and with her.[19]

And what could be more comforting than a cookie and a dream? Twenty-year-old homemaker Debbie Fields was the first in a long line of foodies gone famous. Fields took a beloved dessert, the chocolate chip cookie, made it her own, and successfully placed it in literally every mall-based venue imaginable.[20] Entrepreneurs demonstrate how sound intuition is the enabler for moving from invention to leadership and, ultimately, to megasuccess.

More interesting, though, is the recent formal characterization of female entrepreneurs as "the new power girls." The U.S. Small Business Administration reports women entrepreneurs as one of the top-growing business-owner groups, with a marked and steady increase over the past 20 years. The number of women entrepreneurs now stands at 30 percent of all entrepreneurs, and the numbers are continuing to climb. Women-owned businesses overall are at roughly 23 percent of all U.S. firms.[21] Proud to be one of the new power girls myself, I can personally attest to the fact that women have gone from the furious pursuit of our place in traditional workplace settings to recognition of the strong suits we inherently possess that propel us as actual creators of a unique business. My aim in establishing my leadership institute was to provide executive development services in a way that would give us the most unique advantage possible both in why our clients would choose and remain with us and in the freedom of how we work. This growing "girls' club," as it is now referred to, is a direct outgrowth of how women have come together to recognize, garner, and leverage educational and cultural capability that is in fact most precisely intuition-based.

Indra Nooyi

Indra Nooyi is the chief executive officer (CEO) of PepsiCo. Nooyi is PepsiCo's first female CEO. In 2008 she was listed among *Time* magazine's

World's Most Influential Women and that same year ranked number three in *Forbes*'s listing of the Most Powerful Women. In *Fortune* magazine's ranking of the Most Powerful Women in Business, Nooyi was ranked in the number-one slot in 2006, 2007, and 2008. She has held her current job for the past 5 years. Nooyi's focus is in leading the company toward healthier foods while also helping PepsiCo reduce its internal energy consumption.

As Nooyi assumed her number-three place in this year's *Financial Times* listing of Women at the Top, she was quoted as saying, "Don't ever think you've arrived, and remember that what you don't know is much more than what you do."[22] These are the potent and proactive words of a true intuitive and precisely the persona you want leading your organization's efforts to a sustainable future. The aspect of intuition that looks more at what is to be discovered than at what presently and tangibly exists reflects someone with an open mind and a sixth sense for what is yet to be uncovered. A leader such as Nooyi is well positioned to take in concrete information but to also look for cues for what she can read from the landscape. Such a perceptive skill set comes from acute awareness of what is, enabling her to start with far more information than those around her. From that solid data grasp, such a leader can more clearly see patterns and trends—what works and what doesn't. Potential threats and opportunities become equally more apparent. In Nooyi's case, when she makes her tough calls, she is likely to net the business favorable outcomes.

When Nooyi came to PepsiCo in 1994, she was their senior vice president of strategic planning, directing the organization's global strategy. In 2000 she was promoted to CFO. In both roles, Nooyi had to rely directly on her ability to envision outcomes and directions. Known for her ability to quickly size up situations and react with her brand of candor about what will and won't work, she was able to in each of these pivotal assignments, set keen directions regarding acquisitions and new business ventures. More recently as CEO Nooyi continues to move the company in brand-enhancing directions and when faced with the economic downturn, Nooyi responds tenaciously and in balanced fashion with a blend of process improvements and emerging market expansions. Nooyi's leadership moves throughout her tenure at PepsiCo reflect the actions of an intuitively savvy proactive leader.[23]

FROM THINKING TO DOING

In the examples given of intuitive exemplars, we see individuals whose starting point is clearly and decidedly in right-brain vision and wisdom. What Lagarde and Nooyi in particular share is their insightful awareness of their operating contexts, the ability to think proactively, and a knack for recognizing trends and patterns. In Lagarde's role, this gives her a particular edge in complex negotiations. It enables her to better influence steadfast powers toward a new direction. Furthermore, she is able to more clearly determine where the lines of responsibility for all involved must be drawn. For Nooyi, her big-picture vision enables her to best manage her company's present while adeptly growing its future. The entrepreneurs that were cited have shaped how we live our lives, and we are better individually and collectively for it. Through their inventions, their business models, and most distinctively through their civic contributions, women's entrepreneurial spirit is the embodiment of the feminine leadership brand.

The feminine leadership trait of intuitive thinking with its multiple additive dimensions provides a solid base for what follows. With a woman's intuition as our starting point, we fully leverage our right brain as it was intended—to provide us with the necessary foresight to forge ahead. The next logical step is successful implementation: how we move from right-brain insight to left-brain action. The directive force women have honed is steeped in the notion that once you decide that something is possible, you can and will accomplish what you set out to do.

CHAPTER 3

A WOMAN'S DIRECTIVE FORCE

Look at a day when you are supremely satisfied at the end. It's not a day when you lounge around doing nothing; it's when you've had everything to do, and you've done it.

—Margaret Thatcher[1]

GETTING IT DONE

Reading the above quote from England's first and only female prime minister, Margaret Thatcher, there is no doubt of Thatcher's view. For Thatcher, life is about purposeful accomplishment—a great day is marked by challenges that are met; the more supreme the endeavor, the more satisfying the achievement. The second feminine leadership trait, directive force, reflects just that. Men and women alike are drawn to achieve. The masculine and feminine contexts for achievement, though, tend to differ. Feminine directive force is marked by a collective focus, whereas its masculine counterpart is more individually geared. These underpinnings relate precisely to sociocultural mores; men have historically been reared with primal survival matters in mind, to achieve independently and competitively in order to protect themselves and their loved ones. Women, on the other hand, were reared to nurture.

As nurturers of others, women grew to more naturally think of accomplishment and problem solving as it relates to their caretaking sphere. Women have had to respond to matters of necessity for others. Reacting maternally to the needs of an infant, for example, involves responsiveness in the moment, putting one's own needs second. Caring for a family unit requires

constant management of multiple diverse issues that more often than not cannot wait. As women evolved to take on professional roles, their approaches
toward work were shaped by centuries of collective functioning. Such social
conditioning makes women more natural team leaders and team members.
Add to this the circumstance of women's rights, namely that women have
had to fight for personal and professional freedom and parity. Women have
routinely had to accomplish more and fight harder just to be acknowledged.
Their determination to come from oppression, coupled with a caretaking
premise, creates proclivities in women for a "doing" that is a brand all its
own. Feminine directive force marks a key leadership trait we need to especially capitalize on in this day and age. We see the problems that have
occurred as the masculine emphasis on individuals at the expense of the whole
has gone unchecked for far too long. The pendulum needs to swing and set in
the middle in order for us to continue to advance and thrive in a manner that is
both sustainable and moral.

I was recently visiting a friend. She is a highly regarded marketing executive, flawless at her job. At home, she has a husband who also has a successful
career and two young children. That day she was preparing to leave on a short
business trip. She methodically compiled a detailed set of instructions for the
sitter and for her husband and was doing all she could in advance for the
children—laying out clothing, preparing foods, assembling the various
school-required accoutrements, and tending to their emotional concerns
about her being away. She took phone calls from the office and made a final
post to her Facebook page. I watched as she juggled her commitments. Her
son landed on her lap as she answered the last-minute barrage of work emails
and reached at the very end for items to place in her own suitcase.

Her husband is a great guy and quite an involved dad. She can count on
him to do more than his part. Still, though, my friend's dry sense of humor
relayed a poignant reality as she jokingly whispered to me, "I better not
get hit by a bus because no one else could deal with all of this." We laughed
as she finished getting ready in her "no stone left unturned" way. Her feminine directive force was in full swing and fully evident in the way in which
she addressed her work and life responsibilities. Literally every effort was
empathically based and followed by sound team leadership and guidance.
Her overall aim was to ensure that all core matters were addressed with
understanding, foresight, capability, and tenacity. This is what typifies feminine directive force.

A few weeks later I was facilitating a leadership team meeting with a sharp
group of clients. We were working on their business strategy. The group was
mixed in gender, age, and functional background. As the session unfolded, two
drivers emerged. They were the more senior women in the room. I watched

closely as the two moved fluidly, pushing others to complete our task. It was not so much their boldness that struck me but the nature of their forward momentum. They demonstrated attuned foresight regarding where the team needed to go and layered that with free-flowing brainstorming. They provided factual context while doing what they could to open up the discussion, considering things from multiple angles. Their mission was to get done what we came to do as creatively as possible. Innovative spirit is yet another key ingredient in feminine directive force. An outgrowth of the right-brain intuition described earlier, creativity is not only a component of feminine directive force but a crucial differentiator. Watch women as they are discussing a problem. They naturally free-associate and then seamlessly move to left-brained, structured orchestration. They go from a divergent (open-ended) mindset to a convergent (pragmatically based) one.

What we can glimpse from these two examples is the result of decades of slow yet steady leadership evolution as women expanded beyond their caretaker role into the workforce. Women are now able to carefully position themselves, push harder still, execute, problem solve, and direct with a potent blend of method, innovation, concern, and determination As women continue to forge this unique leadership path, they give their brains an Olympic workout of sorts for complex task accomplishment. This journey began for women as a means of ensuring the well-being of others. As they moved to professional roles, they took with them their fundamental directive traits and assimilated them into their enhanced sociocultural existence. The net result is empathy-based, detailed persistence combined with creative realism. Through centuries of intrinsic evolution, the leadership trait of directive force has been cultivated into its present-day form.

There is a final and perhaps most interesting feature to the feminine brand of stick-to-itiveness. Different from masculine goal-directedness, feminine directive force is rooted in the outcome itself rather than in the person behind the outcome. Mention was made earlier of the view that the feminine brand of accomplishment as it is referenced herein is more communal; it stresses caring for others while its traditional masculine counterpart places emphasis on individual accomplishment. Put another way, the feminine form can be seen as meritocracy-based, while the masculine form is more self-promoting. This is not meant to imply that all directive men are out for themselves and all directive women are altruistic. Rather, it suggests that the social underpinnings for masculine accomplishment stress the advancement of the person while feminine casting for the same trait stresses results and interpersonal impacts. If we look to the psychology of moral development we can find support for this premise.

MORAL UNDERPINNINGS

The original theory on moral development was postulated by Jean Piaget. Piaget is regarded as one of the top developmental psychologists of the twentieth century. Piaget's beliefs stemmed from a biologic view, namely that we mature through distinct cognitive stages based on biologically predetermined programming. In essence, as our brains develop throughout childhood and adolescence, we become more able to move from simple to complex reasoning. Piaget's theory on moral development is an outgrowth of that developmental progression, suggesting that morals are an aspect of development based on our actions and resulting cognitive interpretations of those actions. As a child ages, his or her moral development matures as well and is constructed by virtue of his or her interpersonal relationships and fairness.

Lawrence Kohlberg then came along and focused his studies directly on moral development. Kohlberg in essence extended Piaget's thinking by hypothesizing that moral development was a slower and more extended process continuing on into adulthood. Kohlberg's theory involved three primary levels and six total stages within those levels. He believed that both men and women move through these universal stages similarly. Kohlberg identified fairness as the overarching moral determinant. Kohlberg's six stages are summarized thus:

- At Stage 1, an individual's moral behavior is based on following rules in order to avoid punishment.
- At Stage 2, we begin to see the notion of reciprocity in one's moral thinking—if you watch out for me, I will watch out for you, or if you do something to me, I can reciprocate. There is an exchange-based view here, but mostly what is right or wrong is relative as seen through an individual's personal lens.
- At Stage 3, we begin to think more in terms of the collective. We now think about right and wrong as it impacts those closest to us. Our moral thinking is culturally based, if you will; it is based on what we know from our families and community.
- At Stage 4, we make the shift over to our greater social system. We see ourselves as a member of society, and even when we don't agree, we comply because it is required by the greater system. We do so not simply to avoid official retribution (i.e., punishment for breaking the law) but because we realize that we must support the greater society in order for true order to prevail. In Stage 4, one may begin to consider extreme cases where exceptions to conventional morality may apply—when, for example, the actual law conflicts with a higher social imperative.
- At Stage 5, we continue to apply exceptional thinking and can interpret certain aspects of existing societal rules more qualitatively from the standpoint of reasoning and ultimate morality. We are more interested in acting

    on the basis of the underlying principles that created our rules than on the
    letter of the law, so to speak.
- At Stage 6, moral judgment looks at existing norms, rules, and cultural
perspectives and at the current context and asks, "What do we need to create
and what do we need to become to address humankind's concerns of our
day?"[2]

In the 1980s, a second moral-development theorist, Carol Gilligan, coun-
tered Kohlberg's premise. In particular, Gilligan believed there to be distinct
differences between the genders with respect to morality. Gilligan's view is
widely held today. She believes that men and women have differing impressions of morality. Gilligan relayed that men's morality is, as Kohlberg
believes, based on social justice; however, women have a morality based on
social care. There are two critical elements to Gilligan's thinking that warrant
careful consideration here. The first is that morality based on care is rooted in
nonviolence. The second is that unlike morality based on justice, which says
"treat others fairly," morality based on care says that we should not turn away
from someone in need. Gilligan's view is that females who are reared to identify with their mothers would, as a result of that identification exposure,
ascribe morality as communal. Because men are socialized to separate from
their primary attachment figure, they would look at morality as coordinated
actions by separate individuals.

Gilligan would cite the developmental perspective of identification as an
explanation for why females grow into a more formal care-based moral orientation while men grow into one of fairness. Girls' attachment to and identification with their mothers continues and in fact strengthens as a girl ages. Boys,
on the other hand, more typically separate developmentally from maternal
attachment in order to form their masculine identity. When they do so, it calls
attention to a power differential in relationships (between children and adults)
and attunes the child more to the notion of inequality. Hence the child is more
disposed to think in terms of justice and fairness. Young girls, however, are
not provoked in a similar manner as their attachment remains constant.[3]

The care-versus-justice moral distinction put forth by Gilligan reinforces
how socially etched certain orientations are between men and women and how
there is carry-over to the leadership arena, where both groups are represented
but far from integrated. A concerted effort to represent both masculine and feminine leadership social values will only serve to broaden and strengthen the reach
of leadership overall. The fact that in many ways society has become more
androgynous is a move in that direction. For now we can say that a feminine distinction in directive force is a novel leadership trait and one that in today's world
has vast applicability, especially with respect to team and unity efforts.

There are numerous examples of the misuse or overuse of masculine-rooted directive force. Sadly, the U.S. political system as it functions today is one of them. With the myriad of problems the nation faces, masculine-rooted directive force typifies how the two parties interact. Each side is driving its position on what it believes to be right. Feminine directive force would focus instead on the issues of societal care and repair from a bilateral relationship view. While most politicians would tell you that intellectually they are aligned with the feminine way of thinking—that they are in essence there to serve and are looking for bipartisan solutions—the traditional cultural hard-wiring of our political system (the justice-based moral view) has the players and our country in its grips.

Look again at the economic strife gripping us globally. While countries slip into bankruptcy, they still fight to hold onto what they believe is "fair" for them. As regimes in the Middle East topple, civil war ensues—each side vying for justice, destroying cultures and communities and slaughtering masses instead of caring for those rightly seeking basic human rights. We as a people seem desensitized to violence and inhumanity. Feminine directive force would reverse these harsh ways and bring the feeling back into a paralyzed set of cultures and subcultures. Frankly, putting women in ruling positions would begin to move us in new and healing moral and civil directions. Still, though, we resist. In the United States, for example, supposedly one of the most progressive of nations, we have yet to elect a woman to the highest offices. For that matter, far more female representation is needed at all levels of government.

Interestingly enough, someone with an evolved leadership style and a blended moral view is in the highest office in the United States today. Barack Obama represents a moral philosophy of both care and justice. He is the androgynous leader we are seeking. Obama was elected because he was able to speak the masculine language infused with needed feminine perspectives. Look, though, at the resistance he has faced. His is one of the most contested presidencies in history and all because he is attempting to instill a more balanced moral orientation. Those who continue to look out for their own interests are at fierce odds with that direction. In order to change the current outcome, both the culture and players would have to be called out and made to make the necessary shift. We would need more men and women with dual mindsets to unite and drive the shift.

As I am writing this, news came in from the 2012 Olympics relevant to our morality discussion. South Korean fencer Shin A. Lam apparently refused an Olympic consolidation medal and staged a tearful one-hour protest when a malfunctioning clock enabled her German opponent to score extra points as the match was to end. The German fencer then was awarded what, in Lam's mind, should have been Lam's medal. The news further reported that fencing officials acknowledged the error but said there was nothing they could do about it; they would have to abide by the rules that look to the clock as the ultimate authority.[4] Kohlberg's Stage 4 rule-based fairness principles would agree that we must look to and follow the rules. Perhaps Kohlberg's higher stages of moral reasoning would consider this situation more qualitatively and thus grant Shin Lam the medal. Certainly Gilligan's moral reasoning based on care would override the broken clock and do what is *humanly right.*

A CALL FOR HIGHER MORAL REASONING

In closing our discussion on the moral underpinnings of directive force, look back for a moment to the last two stages of Kohlberg's moral development theory. In them he states that Stages 5 and 6 are where existing societal rules are viewed more qualitatively from the standpoint of reasoning and ultimate morality. In Stage 5 we seemingly act on the basis of the underlying principles that create our rules rather than on the letter of the law itself. At Stage 6, moral judgment looks at existing norms, rules, and cultural perspectives and at the current context. It asks, "What do we need to create and what do we need to become to address humankind's concerns of our day?" Doesn't this sound a lot like care-based morality? If so, does it mean that moving to care-based morality means evolving higher up in the moral structure? It is an interesting question to consider.

KEY ELEMENTS

With a firm understanding of the developmental underpinnings of feminine directive force, what then are its key elements? Put another way, how would one have to proceed in order to act from this leadership perspective? The key elements to feminine directive force are as follows:

1. *Have an empathic purpose for what you set out to do that is clearly and directly tied to the advancement of those you are accountable to.* At the outset you must be able to articulate how your directive leadership actions and intents are in fact for the betterment of the whole and undertaken from their orientation. Starting from a collective imperative serves as your rudder. It will shape how you move through your work and keep you operating from a communal orientation. You as an individual will also benefit from a job well done. The difference, though, is that the overarching purpose is not about your success but about the impact your success will have on others. While this

may sound quite "Pollyanna," it is actually a simple integrity issue in leadership that we have gotten away from—that leadership is about stewardship.

2. *Put a realistic plan in place.* Next give considerable effort to the nature of your plan, process systems, and means. Often we jump in without a solidly constructed structure in place, and things begin to deteriorate from there. The scope of what you set out to do needs to be doable within respect to time frame, context, and resources at your disposal. Your team, those who will be working with you on the project, are another crucial indicator of your outcome. Know their capability and protect yourself against your weakest links. If necessary, eliminate those who aren't going to be able to do what is expected of them. Your strong players are also your coaches and ambassadors—they will not only be instrumental in doing their fair share but in bringing along the less adept members. Ensure that everyone has a voice and a charge. With respect to processes and systems, strike the right balance between accountabilities and supports, but don't be laden down with unnecessary bureaucracy.

3. *Drive hard and don't back down under pressure.* Once you begin, you need to see things through. Address resistance directly and in a straightforward manner, helping those around you feel secure in what you expect and what they stand to gain.

4. *Be nimble, open, and creative.* As much as you need tenacity to get to where you want to be, there is nothing more damaging or dangerous than blind force. Be open to what is going on around you and be willing to make changes and corrections as needed. Most importantly, be willing to take a step back at certain key junctures, away from your left-brain determination, and engage your right-brain creativity, especially when you seemingly hit a wall. There will be more said about this right-brain style switch. A toolkit will be presented later in the chapter that contains vehicles to bolster right- and left-brain transitions. For now, keep in mind the importance of reflection and the ability to think outside of existing parameters in order to find the best possible solutions.

5. *Stay true to your original intent.* Just as you began with a moral premise, you must end with one as well. Examine closely what you delivered and communicate openly and directly if outcomes fell short or were altered from the original intent. Be accountable and a true steward.

ASSERTIVENESS: THE GOOD, THE BAD, AND THE ABSURD

Assertiveness is a key aspect of being directive. To be assertive, one would act in a manner that is upfront, direct, and determined in order to get the desired result. More specifically, you can think of assertiveness in terms of 10 discrete traits, as follows:

- *Purposeful*—being determined and definite in your goals
- *Confident*—being assured about your capability to reach desired goals

- *Tenacious*—being unrelenting
- *Driven*—staying determined to reach goals and get results
- *Delegating*—able to assign and resource the work appropriately
- *Decisive*—able to make sound decisions
- *Courageous*—being willing to face challenges and difficulties
- *Candid*—being upfront and direct
- *Confrontational*—able to work through a conflict
- *Closure-seeking*—seeing things through and pushing for conclusions[5]

Assertive leadership is often contorted, especially in today's high-pressured climate. There is an increasing pattern of micromanaging and harshness, the morphed version of assertiveness that should not be considered positive, assertive leading. Positive, assertive leading is about being in charge in order to reach a goal and doing so in such a way that is professional, intelligent, and ethical. It is not about running over the top of people, being rude or aggressive, or putting your needs ahead of others'. Those who are truly assertive act with resolve. One can be strong, self-assured, and even pushy, aggressive, and brazen at times if what we mean by these particular terms is someone who is willing to act boldly and to make the first move.

Assertive leadership does not include a Machiavellian perspective where the ends justify the means. Attacking without provocation, driving hidden agendas, and acting from arrogance, disrespect, or volatility are also excluded from this leadership view of assertive actions. Your simple gut-check for assertiveness run amok is whether or not your behavior is devaluing, dishonest, or certainly inhumane.[6] This seems fairly straightforward, doesn't it? Yet you would be surprised how many of those in power continue to act badly under the guise of being an assertive leader. Let's look more closely at the distinctions.

What, then, does good, assertive leadership look like? Across the globe, Vice Premier Wu Yi worked to lead her country through unprecedented growth in the face of mammoth challenges. One of four vice premiers for the People's Republic of China, Wu Yi's role is seated in the economy. With a long and distinguished leadership record, Wu Yi's positions have included deputy mayor of Beijing, deputy minister of foreign economic relations and trade, minister of international trade and economic cooperation, and now vice premier. Her winning combination is said to be her unyielding character and definitive stance, hallmarks of an assertive leader. Yi was recognized by *Time* magazine as one of the 100 Most Influential People of 2004 for her courageous and decisive leadership during the severe acute respiratory syndrome (SARS) crisis. *Time* referred to her as the "goddess of transparency" for her candid confrontation of the crisis. More recently, she was named second among *Forbes* magazine's Most Powerful Women in the World. *Forbes* notes both her purposeful involvement internationally and her closure-seeking stance in continuing to assist China through its internal issues and opportunities. At home, Wu Yi's drive, confidence, and tenacity netted her the media nickname "iron lady of China." We can only assume that in accomplishing what she has, Wu Yi is also a sound delegator, able to assign tasks and involve others in the most effective way. As fierce as Wu Yi has been described, we see little if any evidence in her descriptions of being ill mannered or aggressive per se. She is seen as tough, capable, and unstoppable in the appropriate sense of those words.[7]

In the brief description above, Wu Yi can be noted as exemplifying at least 9 of the 10 traits of a positive, assertive leader. She acts with purpose and is self-assured and relentless. She is determined and decisive, acts with courage and candor, and adroitly addresses conflict in an environment where such behavior handled without delicacy could easily be seen as blasphemous. Lastly she is a closer, the final litmus test for the assertive.

Who else could we identify as a positive, assertive exemplar? Christine Lagarde, mentioned previously for her intuitive strong suits, certainly qualifies. Lagarde leverages her intuitive know-how to guide her in recognizing the best possible moments to direct, set limits, and push for accountabilities. Either adeptness alone would have an impact, but working in concert, Lagarde's combined intuition and directive force enable her to decide, then confront and address, what is needed in order to reach workable solutions. Lagarde is also noted in particular as possessing as one of her hallmarks her own brand of candor. This was evident when on July 10, 2007, as newly appointed finance minister of France, she addressed Parliament for the first time and declared to the group that it was time for France to move from thinking to acting. Lagarde cut right to the heart of the matters at hand, calling into question the highly prized French value of contemplation. Many were shocked by Lagarde's brazen declaration. Lagarde reported in an interview with the U.S.-based television show *60 Minutes* that her intent was to motivate.[8] Looking at how she carries herself, communicates, and leads, Lagarde is a role model for what good assertiveness looks like.

Assertive Counterbalance

What, then, does it look like when assertiveness is carried out in a less-than-effective fashion? Assertiveness needs to be balanced in order to be truly effective. A quote by former prime minister Margaret Thatcher started off this chapter on directive force. Thatcher would certainly be considered a positive assertiveness model in many ways. Much of her time in office was a clear illustration of assertive leadership. But Thatcher did have an assertiveness issue. She was, it is true, assertive to a fault. She seemed, over the course of her time in power, unable to balance out her style. Eventually, her assertive manner worked to her detriment. It became an overplayed strength.

Early in her tenure as prime minister, Thatcher set out to effect change in England's socioeconomic and political structures, and more than any other British leaders of her time, she accomplished just that. Her three terms in office were marked by unprecedented reform. Thatcher was seen overall as highly successful. She was also deeply contested by many. She persevered often and repeatedly in the face of her opposition. Much of what she was attempting required the full force of all 10 assertive leadership traits, and Thatcher, more than most, delivered potently on all 10 trait fronts. A popular quote by Thatcher, "Being powerful is like being a lady. If you have to tell people you are, you aren't," succinctly communicates her position.[9] It is quite remarkable that she rose to power in the face of double standard/double bind ridicule. Still she persevered, overcoming those who sought to quell her. She maintained her forceful persona, expecting to be judged as an equal to her male colleagues.

When Thatcher took office in 1979, aggressive measures seemed necessary in order to reverse Britain's rooted economic decline. A conservative, Thatcher took aim on labor unions and indirect taxes. She worked for the privatization of government-run companies and worked to make labor markets operate with more flexibility. Thatcher took a hard line on all forms of terrorism. In response, in 1984 the Irish Republican Army attempted to assassinate Thatcher along with members of her cabinet in a perilous hotel bombing. She pressed on in unwavering fashion. On the foreign policy front, she brought Britain to war in the Falkland Islands when diplomatic options were exhausted. Boldly, Thatcher held steadfast in her public objections to communism. As the Cold War ended and efforts turned to the forming of a European community, Thatcher's views moved from support of the European Union to one of skepticism. This political position would prove to be the breaking point between Thatcher and her party. While many would privately side with her views, Thatcher's blatant determinism left her without key support from those around her.

While she was on the one hand praised for strengthening the British economy and for reshaping how Britain was perceived as a world power, opposition to her deemed stubborn style and tactics continued to mount. In 1986, Thatcher was openly challenged when her defense minister resigned. This seemed the beginning of her demise. She was elected to a third term in 1987, but in 1990 Prime Minister Thatcher resigned when publically challenged by her party.[10]

Like all strong-suits, balance is required in order to be most effective. You have heard the phrase "too much of a good thing." That is precisely what one has to guard against in leadership and in life. At a certain point, one's assets can be expressed to excess. The result is ultimate failure. Leaders must maintain certain counterbalances so as not compromise their overall impact. In Thatcher's case, her assertiveness, while mostly and perhaps sorely needed during much of her reign, required a bit of finessing. Thatcher needed to display a formidable nature in the context of the political landscape she operated from. In Thatcher's case, she was under-political—looking solely at and for the collective outcomes and what was, in her mind, in the best interest of her people. She needed to pay attention to her political context. One downside of strong feminine-based assertiveness is that the politics operating around you can sometimes be ignored. Politics are seen as self-serving and therefore can be minimized in importance. The fact of the matter is that there is a political element to everything leaders seek to accomplish, and one must attend to politics in order to avoid being thwarted.

Organizationally savvy authors Rick Brandon and Marty Seldman were initially referenced in Chapter 2 in the section on awareness. Specifically, one needs to guard against those who are overly political so that their hidden agendas don't blind-side you in your efforts. Thatcher was under pressure and was blind-sided by her opposition. To provide a more complete view of Brandon and Seldman's perspective, they identify four political styles for leaders to consider. At the far ends of their continuum are the under-political and the overly political. The under-political tend too much to the collective; they look to their mission to the exclusion of politics. The overly political are seen as self-serving to excess, concerned with what their accomplishments do to advance them personally. The two styles in the middle, the less and the more political, occupy what Brandon and Seldman call the savvy zone. Those who fall into this savvy zone are referred to as having *impact with integrity*. Anyone operating at one extreme or the other is encouraged to move to the middle in order to operate from uprightness while still tending to those whose support they need.[11]

Abuses of Power

Learning to better balance your assertiveness by becoming more appropriately savvy is a workable developmental goal for a leader who strays too far in one direction or the other. Assertiveness to excess, though, can take on a more egregious form and result in a direct abuse of power. Described earlier as leadership gone amok, here we witness everything from increasing patterns of micromanaging and harshness to those who, more often than not, run over the top of others, are rude, and are self-aggrandizing. In their worst form, abuses of power are criminal in nature where others are harmed, victimized, or obliterated. It is unfortunate to say that a full range of power abuses is far more common than we would fathom even in seemingly civilized settings. It appears over time we are becoming almost desensitized to many of the infractions when, as an evolving people, the opposite should be the case.

In the 1990s in U.S. business, Al Dunlap, former Sunbeam and Scott Paper head, employed notorious methods to see to it that business goals were met. Dunlap was nicknamed "Chainsaw Al" and "Rambo in Pinstripes" for his merciless tactics, downsizing being his hallmark leadership play. He was voted one of *Time* magazine's Top Ten Worst Bosses, yet Dunlop stood by his own tactics, detailing them in a work entitled *Mean Business.* In 1998, Dunlop's bad behavior caught up with him, and he was eventually let go.[12] Still, today downsizing at least is an acceptable and often overapplied leadership practice for meeting fiscal targets. While no doubt there are times when restructuring is necessary for business solvency, it should be something leaders consider long and hard relative to its human impacts and as a last resort. Instead it often seems a first reaction to difficult times. What about the Catholic Church's handling of uncovered sexual abuses by some of its priests? Was its response to the problem acceptable? Consider the scandal that ensued when U.S. presidential hopeful John Edwards was accused of using campaign funds to cover up an extramarital affair during his 2008 campaign. While Edwards's trial resulted in a mistrial and he was acquitted on the one charge he was prosecuted on, Edwards is one in a long line of public officials whose use of power has been called into question.

Individuals like Bernard Madoff, a former American businessman who perpetuated a Ponzi scheme that is considered to be the largest financial fraud in U.S. history, fit this bill. Think of the damage Madoff's crime had on the individual victims. He was prosecuted and sent to prison, but what of the many individuals responsible in one way or another for the overall mortgage collapse? Are we satisfied that they were held accountable? That list could go on and on. Even everyday individuals in positions of power act badly. Many are caught and fired, but many are left to act as they do. We seem somehow resigned to the fact that this is just the way that it is. Something seems fundamentally off in our cultural values, something a feminine orientation would have far less patience for.

Adolf Hitler was surely the worst-case power criminal in modern times. Rulers like Libya's Muammar Gaddafi were only recently brought down. African cult leader Joseph Kony reportedly ordered the abduction of tens of thousands of children to become child sex slaves and child soldiers. What do we think of that? How many others can you name, individuals who today have

enormous power and are doing immense harm? How will we *resensitize* ourselves? How will we bring care and concern back? How can each of us lead differently in order to recast power? What should each of us no longer tolerate in
others or in ourselves? These are just a few important questions to consider
about the true nature of might from the feminine camp.

Facts and Assumptions: A Final Assertive Consideration

Assertiveness is a potent dimension of directive leadership. It helps instill
confidence in those being led. When our leaders act from positive assertive
principles it is one indicator that we are in good hands. We admire those
who are determined, purposeful, and able to get things done. We feel
reassured by those who speak up and speak out to represent our best interests.
Such insistent character traits can be perceived by some as charismatic, while
others see the diligent as relatable, down-to-earth, and hands on in a good
way. This array of impressions is precisely what many experienced when
vice-presidential candidate Sarah Palin took the 2008 election by storm.
Palin, then governor of Alaska, was not only a fresh face but possessed an
uncanny appeal as a self-made professional woman and mother. She had guts,
was outspoken, and seemed to be able to accomplish anything she set her mind
to. Palin came out swinging with a refreshingly bold, assertive style that was
initially captivating. What made her appeal all the more convincing was that
she seemed to be a basic, hardworking person who came up through the ranks
and was now about to realize the next American dream. She was poised to
become the first woman in the number-two spot in the White House. Palin
came close to joining the honored collection of women who reached 1600
Pennsylvania Avenue, but not as a Cabinet member, a first lady, or a high-
ranking staffer—as the vice president of the United States.

What, though, went wrong? How did Sarah Palin fall from grace? Palin
exhibited a dangerous assertiveness flaw, the inability to separate fact from
assumption in expressing one's resolve. She spoke out on matters of great
importance but often with unfounded views, erroneous logic, or incorrect information. A fact is something that is proven, a piece of data that has been objec-
tively substantiated: Today's temperature outside, as measured by a working
thermometer, is 87 degrees. In the 112th U.S. Congress there were 362 men
and 76 women in the House and 17 women and 83 men in the Senate.[13]

An assumption, on the other hand, is something believed without actual
proof. In order to operate from sound and reputable directive leadership, one
needs to speak with these distinctions clearly in mind. If you don't, you are
in essence running away with your thoughts. One begin making connections
that are baseless. Liberties in communication are taken that quickly and often

irreversibly diminish credibility. At best one appears to overgeneralize. The most damaging result is that you are perceived as ill equipped to lead in a given role. When Palin made her first communication gaff, it was during a televised interview with ABC News correspondent Charles Gibson, who asked Palin what insights she had from her state being in such close physical proximity to Russia. She responded: "They're our next-door neighbors, and you can actually see Russia from land here in Alaska, from an island in Alaska."[14] In a perfect world, this would have been an interesting initial data point and what would follow would have been more facts about her actual foreign policy experiences, exposures, or limitations. When she was pressed further in a follow-up interview with Katie Couric, this was the dialogue:

Couric: You've cited Alaska's proximity to Russia as part of your foreign policy experience. What did you mean by that?

Palin: That Alaska has a very narrow maritime border between a foreign country, Russia, and on our other side, the land—boundary that we have with—Canada. It—it's funny that a comment like that was—kind of made to—I don't know, you know? Reporters—

Couric: Mock?

Palin: Yeah, mocked, I guess that's the word, yeah.

Couric: Explain to me why that enhances your foreign policy credentials.

Palin: Well, it certainly does because our—our next door neighbors are foreign countries. They're in the state that I am the executive of. And there in Russia—

Couric: Have you ever been involved with any negotiations, for example, with the Russians?

Palin: We have trade missions back and forth. We—we do—it's very important when you consider even national security issues with Russia as Putin rears his head and comes into the air space of the United States of America, where—where do they go? It's Alaska. It's just right over the border. It is—from Alaska that we send those out to make sure that an eye is being kept on this very powerful nation, Russia, because they are right there. They are right next to—to our state.[15]

The ensuing media firestorm criticized the high-profile Palin for a loosely constructed argument that seemed unable to provide substance to back her position. Proximity and peripheral exposure does not translate to specific foreign policy experience or know-how. As the campaign pressed on, we heard more strong opinions from Palin that lacked factual and experiential substance to back them. Assumptions seemed the majority of her thought pattern, with a noticeable absence of relevant intellectually founded data backing them.

You recall that the first key trait in the IDEA-based leadership model is intuition, and intuition is actually an assumption. Leaders should initiate their thinking in the right brain with intuitive thinking. The leader's mind then should move to left-brain analytics where actual data and facts are synthesized to support or refute what is supposed. Assumption sans substantiation is little more than a bias. If someone like Palin relies solely on the skills and information she has in one constricted arena and then applies that knowledge to a far more complex circumstance, she will be woefully underprepared to leverage a cogent premise.

Noted political satirist Bill Mahr refers to this propensity for treating assumptions as facts as *living in the bubble*. Mahr explains that you tend to create a world of limited, inaccurate, or unfounded points and call it gospel. The world then exists in your *bubble*. The bubble is your reality, not actual reality. Those who confuse fact and assumption are known to fiercely preach views and are far less inclined to learn new facts, especially when those facts counter their existing position. In Palin's defense, the precipitous move she was expected to make from where she was as governor of Alaska to the global role of vice presidential candidate was significant. Had she perhaps afforded herself more of a learning curve, there could have been a different outcome. She could have shown us her assertive strong suits and, at least initially, held back on her opinions until she came up to speed. Seeing her as a good student and quick learner, the media may have had patience with her as she assimilated fully into the campaign. A sound assertive leader would have confronted her interviewers, saying she welcomed a second interview with them in the near future to continue the discussion as she more fully made her way into the campaign.

Think for a moment of those you experience who seem to treat fact and assumption as one and the same. How do you see this limiting them? What impact does their tact have on those around them? It is a more common problem than you might think, and one easily remedied by openness to learning. The point here is not to confuse bias-based resolve with sound assertiveness. Sound assertiveness is born of intuition and then backed by factual knowledge.

A DIRECTIVE FORCE TOOLKIT

To recount, the key elements of directive force include

- beginning with empathic purpose
- setting a realistic plan in place
- driving hard (good assertiveness)
- being nimble, open, and creative
- staying true to your original intent

What these components indicate is the need for proficiencies on five fronts. We need to be proficient in gaining openness and understanding, we need to plan well and with creativity, we need to possess well-balanced assertiveness, and, finally, we need to be held accountable for our outcomes.

The favorable aspect of the IDEA-based leadership model is that its traits, skills, and tools build as you move through it. What that means is the three tools taught in Chapter 2 (those that help build intuitive know-how) are foundational to building directive force. Those skills include active listening, clearing your mind, and reflection. Active listening is a crucial aspect of empathy building, the starter proficiency in becoming more open and understanding. Clearing your mind helps you begin your planning process free of distraction and focused on the task at hand. The ability to reflect will be vital to you as you gauge your progress along the way, assess the need for course corrections, and ultimately determine how true you are to your original intent.

Moving to our five new skills, how can we further build *open understanding*? Open understanding begins with a mindset receptive to curiosity and exploration. We need to be truly interested in what is novel and unique. Words like *odd, peculiar*, or *strange* need to be put aside and reframed with words like *interesting* and *new*. An activity called extension learning can help. *Extension learning* is an exercise that broadens your knowledge beyond its present scope. Once a week over the next six months, take something you are familiar with and expand beyond it. Do so with something clearly out of your present scope of interest and/or comfort. For example, if you are a "foodie," interested in cooking or dining out as a hobby, once a month try a new cuisine entirely, something you would not necessarily consider or be exposed to. If you work out at the gym and do standard cardio activities or weight training, try a yoga class or some other more inward-based exercise activity. The value of extension learning is that it moves your brain off of its habitual track and encourages open-mindedness. If you try something and you really don't like it, react to it as simply different. Avoid negative thoughts when ascribing meaning to what you've encountered.

Another form of extension learning is the study of cultures. This serves not only to facilitate openness and understanding but can allow you to develop greater empathy. Look online and read about cultures you know little about. You may want to research cultures you have negative assumptions about and see if anything you research helps you understand things better from their perspective or gives a basis for their opposing beliefs. The goal is not about changing your view but about understanding and acknowledging life as they see it, free of judgment.

Planning and *creativity building* are next. There is one tool that facilitates both. That tool is *mind mapping*. Tony Buzan, author of the book *Use Both*

Sides of Your Brain, is the inventor of mind mapping. Buzan explains our innate programming for using both sides of our brain to our planning and creative advantage. The right and left sides of our brain are not simply two connected structures with different characteristics; rather they are two structures each containing facets of the other's abilities. The brain is synergistic; when we encourage the development of a weaker mental area, not only does the weaker area develop but the dominant areas continue to develop as well.[16] Some of us are more disposed to the structured and the methodical (we are planners) while others are more unstructured and creative. Here we have an activity that encourages both, thereby bolstering our abilities across the board. Mind mapping enables us to foster directive leadership ability with creative planning as we construct a visual and nonlinear organization of ideas and images around a central thought. Mind maps allow the brain to think more freely and completely. You can learn Buzan's mind mapping technique in his best-selling book *How to Mind Map: Make the Most of Your Mind and Learn to Create, Organize and Plan.*

Drawing is another way to encourage creative planning while it also assists your directive leadership in terms of how you evaluate your plan and understand what needs to be adjusted. The creativity comes from using symbols and colors versus relying on words, lists, or outlines. As you use the right, nonverbal side of your brain and introduce color, creative thought is stimulated. Limiting yourself to left-brain planning and evaluative measures censors and constricts your thinking. Preconceived and habitual notions will dominate. Drawing gets to a freer, unbiased aspect of your thinking.

Take a large piece of flip-chart paper and a box of colored markers. Divide the page in half with a solid line. On the top half, draw your circumstance as it exists today, and on the bottom, draw it as you would like it to be or the result you are hoping for—your end point. Reflect on what you have drawn, and now access the left side of your brain to summarize in writing what you have depicted. This narrative will bring you to an open account of where you are versus where you are headed.

The fourth skill is *assertiveness*. How does one become more tenacious? You accomplish this through the tools of behavior rehearsal and chaining. *Behavior rehearsal* is the structured practice of a new behavior until it is well integrated. *Chaining* is defined as taking progressive steps toward a goal. Put these two tools together for the best result. Start with a situation or a person that would be easiest for you to confront. Practice being more and more direct with less imposing individuals and circumstances and do so until you are completely comfortable. Build up to those to whom you find expressing candid thoughts more difficult. Small, rehearsed steps over time will make you more assertive. The more you repeat this activity while upping the ante, the more direct you will be in how you express yourself.

Something to keep in mind relative to your assertive impact is your nonverbal communication, in particular your tone. Whether you are already comfortable with directness or building your acumen in this area, *tone* is a key determinant of effectiveness. We are under the misconception that we need to be loud or imposing when confronting others in order to show that we mean business. Actually, quite the opposite is true. Let your words speak for themselves when confronting. Keep your emotion low, your tone respectful, and your words firm. You should appear to have a calm, confident persona. That is all that is needed. Exaggerated tonal qualities build defensiveness in your receiver and may mitigate the result you are trying to achieve. The less defensive others are, the more likely they are to hear you and be influenced by you.

The final skill in building directive force is *accountability*. You want to ensure that you hold true to your plan as well as to your original communal intent. Accountability partners and mentors are the keys to that end. An *accountability partner* is a colleague, friend, or family member you trust with whom you can discuss your plan regularly. Doing so ensures that you are on track. Accountability partners should be those who will be open with you (tell it like it is). It is important to realize that they are not mind readers; they are only going to be as good for you as you are honest and complete with them.

Mentors are meant to provide more in the way of wisdom and experience. Look for someone who is at the level you aspire toward or someone whose accomplishment and insight you value. Both mentors and accountability partners are particularly important to those who are seeking to bolster their directive force, but perhaps even more necessary for those who are already highly directive. Those of you who are too assertive need to be kept in check by someone more seasoned. The very fact that you take the step to being better monitored is half the battle.

DIRECTIVE FORCE EXEMPLARS

Business Empire Icons: Martha Stewart and Oprah Winfrey

I found it interesting that in conducting research on the most powerful women, Martha Stewart's name didn't come up as often as you would think. Yet if you Google Martha Stewart products, the numbers would astound you. Tens of thousands of Martha Stewart products would be a conservative estimate. Referred to as a business magnate, lifestyle guru, media personality, and publisher, Stewart's creatively based directive force seems boundless. From the inception of her catering business in the mid-1970s to the early 1990s, Stewart grew her empire to $763 million in annual retail sales. In those less than 20 years, Martha Stewart advanced from a successful entrepreneur and writer to a business icon whose empire included two magazines, a television show, recipe publications, a syndicated newspaper column, a series of how-to books, a radio show, and an Internet site. I get exhausted just reading the list.

Her company, Martha Stewart Living Omnimedia, went public in 1999, and her fame and success continues to the present day. Her estimated worth is now in the billions.[17] Stewart epitomizes directive stature. She is the optimal blend of ingenious creativity and flawless execution. Her attention to detail and ability to make things happen is unmatchable. She is a directive force all her own. Her work is seated in enhancing our everyday living, helping us derive pleasure and satisfaction from what and how we eat along with making our homes a welcoming sanctuary. While some would call her work superficial, it affords us enjoyment and pleasure. Her organizational efficiency bent to all she does instills order, which in these chaotic times is worth it in and of itself. I thought long and hard about whether or not to include Stewart here, especially in light of the fact that she is far from selfless. In that regard, she tends to conduct herself more from a masculine perspective than a feminine one. She also served time in prison for a felony conviction. Believe it or not, these two points are precisely why she must be included. Stewart is an example of a woman who achieved what she did by virtue of her sheer determination. She pushed hard in order to realize her vision, and she did so on her terms. If she were a man, she would have been hailed supreme. As a woman, she was more criticized than not. Those who see her negatively are acting from the very double standard we as aspiring women are working so very hard to mitigate. Thank you, Martha, for forging the path and for all that you have done to bring parity, fun, festivity, and taste into our lives.

A business mogul of a different sort is Oprah Winfrey. Where Winfrey seats herself with respect to her contributions is noteworthy for all, but especially for women, whose interest she has always kept front and center in her work. From humble origins in 1950s rural Mississippi to a Baltimore talk show in 1974, Winfrey's career and place in media history was off and running. Oprah Winfrey's keen insight gave rise to relentless candor as she humanly and empathically brought us face-to-face with the full spectrum of life's everyday struggles in a way that was ethically accessible to the masses. Winfrey's directive force comes from her naturally confrontational style, one that allowed her throughout her distinguished career to address social issues openly and with her brand of well-received straightforwardness. Winfrey's frank style may in part emanate from a deeply personal place. It is reported that Winfrey is a survivor of a most horrific injustice: child sexual abuse. Winfrey's assaults are said to have begun at age nine and were perpetrated by multiple predators, individuals reportedly known to her family and trusted by them. She, like most victims, kept her abuse to herself for many years. As she worked through this trauma and ultimately confronted it, her directive impact was likely fortified and realized. Hers is a story of boldness and courage in its most profound form.[18]

A quote from Winfrey emulating a key element of directive force is, "Luck is a matter of preparation meeting opportunity."[19] A translation would be, "be ready and success will follow." *The Oprah Winfrey Show* was launched in 1986 with an audience of 10 million viewers. Her show grossed $125 million in its first year. Harpo Productions was then formed by Winfrey. Her personal brand became iconic as literally anything she touched turned to gold. Her referent power meant that having an endorsement by Oprah netted instant success. She cofounded Oxygen Media in 1999, a venture dedicated to media programming for women. Now focused on the infamous *O* magazine and the Oprah Winfrey Network, which launched in January of 2011, Oprah continues to be a dynamic social force for everyday women all over the world.[20]

Selfless Activist: Aung San Suu Kyi

Aung San Suu Kyi's story is one that touches us on many levels. We revere her and we ache for her. Hers is a story of selfless directive conviction. She was forced to choose between her cause and her loved ones. She chose personal sacrifice. She endured great risks to her own safety and persevered as she worked unwaveringly to advance democracy for her people. Here is her story. Born in 1945 in Rangoon, Burma, her father, a general, was assassinated when Suu Kyi was just two years old. In 1948, Burma was established as an independent union. Her mother, a prominent social figure, was appointed Burmese ambassador to India in 1960. Suu Kyi moved to New Delhi with her mother and later attended college at Oxford in England and graduate school in the United States. She married Michael Aris in 1972. They lived first in Bhutan, a Himalayan kingdom, and then in England, where their two children were born. Suu Kyi became a writer. In 1988, she relocated to Rangoon to care for her ailing mother, and shortly thereafter the country was engulfed by political turmoil where thousands were killed. Suu Kyi became a democracy activist as she worked methodically and potently to cull forces against their oppression. She was so effective, and perceived as such a threat to the government, that she was arrested without charges or a trial. She remained on house arrest and in seclusion for 15 years as she stood firm for the freedoms of her people.

Suu Kyi was awarded the Nobel Peace Prize in 1991. She donated all $1.3 million in monetary prize to the Burmese liberty cause as she remained on house arrest in Burma. She refused either to leave or to stand down in her opposition to the ruling body. Despite repeated attempts by prominent global figures to have her released or to allow her family to visit, she remained isolated and detained. Her husband died of cancer in 1999. She was not permitted to see him while he was ill. In 2010, Suu Kyi was released and met by a crowd of thousands of supporters and followers.[21] Whenever I recall Suu Kyi's story I get goose bumps. What a brave and powerful woman! Suu Kyi is in my mind the mother of humanity.

Woman of the Century: Eleanor Roosevelt

Eleanor Roosevelt was discussed in Chapter 1 as a formidable female force. As such, her accomplishments and persona beg further mention when we speak of directive force. For more than 30 years, the impeccably self-disciplined and immeasurably compassionate Roosevelt contributed to humankind at home and abroad. She was considered the ultimate liberated woman, and her voice made us do what was civilized and "right."

Noteworthy here is the nature of her assertiveness. It was acquired, not innate. It came as a result of emotional strife and forced necessity. Roosevelt endured great personal loss early in life with the deaths of both parents and a brother. Later she would lose a child as an infant and have to endure the subversion of her maternal role with her remaining children from a fiercely controlling mother-in-law. Her personality inclination was overall more passive, yet when she married the high-profile Franklin Roosevelt, she needed to play a lead role in her social circle, including that of first lady of the United States. Her additional defining moment was when her husband's extramarital affair was exposed. From that point on, while loyal to the marriage, she set out on her separate path.[22]

Many of Roosevelt's accomplishments have been noted earlier. Overall, she sought to empower women, improve their professional conditions and opportunities, and fight for day care, health care, and human rights for all. Hers is certainly a legacy of empathy-based feminine directive force. Roosevelt shows that assertiveness can be learned and rise to its most mighty form in those who seem initially not so inclined. She grew to be the most consummate of ethical stewards. Her quotes below epitomize what feminine directive force encompasses.

> I could not, at any age be content to take my place by the fireside and simply look on. Life was meant to be lived. Curiosity must be kept alive. One must never, for whatever reason, turn one's back on life.[23]
>
> You gain strength, courage and confidence by every experience in which you really stop to look fear in the face. You are able to say to yourself, "I've lived through this horror. I can take the next thing that comes along." You must do the thing you think you cannot do.[24]

Woman of Our Future: Hillary Rodham Clinton

Hillary Rodham Clinton picks up where Eleanor Roosevelt left off. Clinton will be primarily responsible for taking women from where we are to where we need to be. Clinton is a consummate thinker, student, teacher, and leader. If you observe her as she speaks, you will note that her principles are the product of voracious learning and keen empathy. She comes across as both methodical and innovative. Clinton appears tenacious to a fault while possessing an accessible communication tone and demeanor that makes her might palpable in even the most contested of situations. She began her professional involvement immersed in politics and causes. She is an active doer who seeks reform for the betterment of society.

Tracing Clinton's professional history since Yale Law School, her timetable is as follows:

1974—Served as a member of the impeachment inquiry staff advising the judiciary committee during the Watergate Scandal and then taught at the University of Alabama Law School with soon-to-be-husband Bill Clinton.

1975—Married Bill Clinton.

1976—Worked on Jimmy Carter's successful presidential campaign.

1977—Appointed by President Carter to chair the Legal Services Corporation while working at the Rose Law Firm.

1979–1981, 1983–1992—First lady of Arkansas, where Clinton launched numerous initiatives to advance the quality of life for children and families in her state. Clinton also served on the boards of TCBY and Wal-Mart.

1980—Daughter Chelsea was born.

1988 and 1991—Named one of the top 100 most powerful lawyers in America by the *National Law Journal.*

1993—Became first lady of the United States following her husband's election as president. First Lady Clinton was appointed head of the Health Care Reform Task Force by her husband during her tenure as first lady.

1997—Established Vital Voices Democracy with then–secretary of state Madeline Albright in support of a U.S. foreign policy initiative to facilitate the advancement of women.

2001–2009—Served as U.S. senator for the state of New York.

2007—Became a U.S. presidential candidate.

2009—Appointed U.S. secretary of state.

Clinton also authored nine books over the course of her professional life, and more than 100 books have been written about her.[25]

Said to be the most traveled secretary of state in history, Clinton's resilience seems boundless. Not only does she quantitatively log miles with a schedule that many would be hard-pressed to keep up with, but her qualitative outputs are more impressive still, especially given the inexplicable global issues igniting all around us. As secretary of state, Clinton has leveraged her honed communication skills, operational savvy, global socioeconomic and cultural acumen, and human-centric perspectives to advance the office of secretary of state as well as U.S. foreign policy directions. In excerpts from her January 13, 2009, nomination hearing statement to be secretary of state, Clinton had this to say:

> For me, consultation is not a catch-word. It is a commitment. . . . America cannot solve the most pressing problems on our own, and the world cannot solve them without America. The best way to advance America's interest in reducing global threats and seizing global opportunities is to design and implement global solutions. This isn't a philosophical point. This is our reality. . . . I believe that American leadership has been wanting, but is still wanted. We must use what has been called "smart power": the full range of tools at our disposal—diplomatic, economic, military, political, legal, and cultural—picking the right tool, or combination of tools, for each situation. With smart power, diplomacy will be the vanguard of foreign policy. This is not a radical idea. The ancient Roman poet Terence, who was born a slave and rose to become one of the great voices of his time, declared that "in every endeavor, the seemly course for wise men is to try persuasion first." The same truth binds wise women as well.[26]

From her civically active beginnings at Yale Law School to her tumultuous global role as U.S. secretary of state, Clinton's consummate feminine directive force has moved us to enhanced future states. From this vantage point, Clinton's skill and manner of leadership represents the new normal. Her foundational knowledge base and communal orientation coupled with sheer determination gives us a working model for what best practice assertiveness looks like for men and women alike. As such, she represents the future of directive leadership: what we should all aspire to become. Secretary Clinton, we implore you to run for president in 2016!

FEMININE DIRECTIVE FORCE: PARTING THOUGHT

The material presented on feminine directive force illuminates the qualities of leadership intent on accomplishment with a mutual purpose. It calls out how the feminine brand of "doing" differs from the masculine type. The exemplars highlighted herein bring the facets of this key leadership trait to life. Whether business icons, political activists, or governing powers, we saw women whose contributions were grounded in sound assertive practices, creative drive, and a firm empathic grasp.

As more and more women assume higher positions of power, we see greater evidence of favorable directive outcomes. Consider this recent data from a 2008 report by Credit Suisse Research Institute analyzing trends that impact global markets. The particular area under investigation was female representation on corporate boards. The report concluded that companies with women on their boards outperformed male-only boards for companies with market capitalization of more than $10 billion and did so by 26 percent over the six-year period studied. The report was quoted as saying that the influence of women on boards serves to "temper risky investment moves and increase return on equity." The report further noted that additional related academic studies showed the following advantages of mixed-gender boards: better attendance records, more diligent oversight, and greater investment in auditing when business circumstances became more intricate.[27] What do these results tell us?

FROM ASSERTING TO EMPOWERING: BUILDING SUSTAINABLE CHANGE

With our understanding of what it takes to plan, create, and execute clearly in mind, we move to a leadership stance that not only has others' interests in mind but brings them into the fold in a manner that enhances our impact exponentially. Chapter 4 focuses on the third key trait of IDEA-based leadership: empowerment. Empowerment builds and strengthens the involvement, skill, and impact of those around us so that what we direct is not only accomplished in the present day but into the future. Empowerment affords that both the contributions leaders seek to make and the people whose lives those contributions touch are sustained. Through empowerment, we can enhance the abilities, outputs, and opportunities of individuals, work groups, and communities. We can determine and leverage collective strengths. What, then, does empowerment the IDEA way entail?

CHAPTER 4

EMPOWERING INTENT

If you have knowledge, let others light their candles in it.

—Margaret Fuller[1]

Margaret Fuller lived from 1810 to 1850. She was an accomplished writer, journalist, and literary critic as well as an educator and women's rights advocate. Some of her most noteworthy accomplishments are that she was the first woman allowed into the Harvard Library to pursue research, the first woman literary critic who also set literary standards, the first American woman to author a book about equality for women, and the first woman foreign correspondent and war correspondent to serve under combat conditions. Fuller's work and perspectives were positioned to encourage women to confront the very nature of their existence. For Fuller, women needed to provoke a greater role for themselves in society.[2]

My favorite factoid about Fuller is that her provocative demeanor and then perceived radical thinking inspired the creation of the character Hester Prynne in Nathaniel Hawthorne's novel *The Scarlett Letter*. Fuller forged more emancipating mindsets regarding the place of women in society and went a step further as she called into question the manner in which all oppressed groups were treated. Fuller's thought quoted above, "If you have knowledge, let others light their candles in it," aptly conveys the aim of those with empowering intent.

WHAT IT MEANS TO EMPOWER

The word *empower* means to give authority or to make someone more confident. When you empower someone, you give them greater responsibility. You afford them the opportunities to be more and to do more. You enable them to make greater contributions, to enrich that which they are a part of. We empower a child to tie his or her own shoes. We empower a teenager to care for younger siblings. An aspiring worker may be empowered to run a project team, or a supervisor asked to step in for a boss who is away. These are but a few examples of how we extend an individual's reach, entrusting him or her with greater obligation. In order to empower, you must provide a frame; one needs to identify the scope of newly entrusted tasks. When empowering others, it is equally important to determine how best to prepare others to succeed. It is not enough to let go of the control. A sound empowering leader provides key teaching elements and parameters along with the proper guidance to enable others to readily carry forth their tasks.

Empowering leaders vest, endow, allow, encourage, galvanize, and rouse others. If you spend a portion of your leadership day emulating any of these traits, you are empowering. What, then, are the attributes of empowering individuals? What is it about someone that inclines them to energize others? Those who empower have three distinct tendencies. First, they value knowledge, most importantly the sharing of knowledge and the cultivation of shared mastery. Hand-in-hand with one's regard for knowing, those who empower value listening for understanding. The last character trait of those who empower is that they are collectively directed. Empowering individuals more naturally see a connectedness between and among others. That inclination draws them to see beyond themselves. As such, they represent a special group of teachers and mentors. They have a keen sense for culling information in an evaluative manner and brining that perspective into the open so that it now becomes available for use by the group. Their expectation—what is at the forefront of their thinking—is for others to share in the path forward. They are less concerned with immediate gains and more interested in cultivating sustainable future states. They realize that through engaging others and encouraging ownership, you build that which endures. You inherently foster environments of mutuality. Let's look more closely at each attribute of those with empowering intent.

Shared Knowledge and Mastery

At the core of empowering intent is preparation. In order to set someone off on a new path, they must be prepared. They must be ready to safely and successfully take on greater responsibility. Preparation comes through learning, and learning begins with the sharing of knowledge. While I have had many roles and job titles throughout my career and to the present day, I would consider everything I do to be teaching-based. I have taught formally at several colleges; I am a trainer and training designer. I have taught others how to instruct. In my work as a clinician, leader, and consultant, I consider my primary focus pedagogical. I see the role of anyone in an informative capacity as not to impress or to preach but to engage others in their own learning process. Any teaching role is about providing knowledge, questions, and discussions so that others can advance. Those who teach come into scholarship through study, research, practice, and reflection. Those who teach through shared knowledge and mastery seek the best possible interactive ways to facilitate learning. They see themselves as facilitators, encouraging others to become more curious and aware. They drive the comprehension of key facets and concepts through active involvement. They work to help others integrate that information into an expanded perspective. Such teachers use proven theory, techniques, systems, and processes to spur thinking and experiential learning. Experiential learning allows others a trial-and-error process toward eventual mastery.

Feminist writers describe a unique quality pertaining to how women see knowledge and teaching complementary to a shared knowledge and mastery premise. Feminist views stress the direct involvement of the learner in the teaching process through discussion, collaborative group work, and discovery. In the book *Women's Ways of Knowing*, feminist writers Belenky, Clinchy, Goldberger, and Tarule speak about the value of nurturing and imperfection in the learning process. Nurturing engenders interactive teaching and learning. For these authors, the nurturing aspect of teaching involves a genuine connection to others: the feeling learners get from their interactions with you. You demonstrate that you are invested in them, that you want them to do well, and that you are committed to encouraging their development. The "imperfection" piece regards teaching not as an infallible expert conveying wisdom but as the enablement of a knowledge-based discovery process. Belenky, Clinchy, Goldberger, and Tarule write, "So long as teachers hide the imperfect process of their thinking, allowing their students to glimpse only the polished products, students will remain convinced that only Einstein, or the professor, could think up a theory."[3]

What the *Women's Ways of Knowing* collective seeks to stress is a two-fold method for bringing empowerment into the learning process. Whether between a parent and child, in a formal classroom, at a workplace training seminar, or between worker and boss, teaching is not about lecturing to impart knowledge. It is not a game of follow-the-leader but rather an opportunity to share knowledge, perspectives, facts, and theories in such a way that the student is empowered both through his or her process and as a result of it. By emboldening learners as part of their learning, you help them experience newfound autonomy, confidence, and independence as they learn. You prepare them occupationally while strengthening their sense of obligation as well.

Empowering educators bring to bear a framework and system of solid knowledge. They are clearly in command of the greater information piece and the direction and scope of the learning. They then involve the group in order to process what the knowledge conveyed actually means in the context of their learning. Together, educator and students alike grapple with concepts and answer resulting questions, all while shaping themselves and the information presented. No knowledge base is complete or perfect in this regard. If you share knowledge in this manner, you increase the likelihood of deeper comprehension. You further allow for the internalization of learning through the cognitively motivational valuing of the student's input.

Instructors of this nature fluidly ebb and flow among multiple spheres of influence. They are on the one hand exercising their legitimate power (influence by virtue of their position). They are also leveraging the influence they have by virtue of their knowledge base (information) or expertise (skill). Such forms of influence are considered directive. When you add in a form of influence that takes the focus off of the educator and onto the learner (involving), drawing out others and valuing their input, you tap a method of influence that is more about how you make others feel about themselves. Moving forth and back between the directive and the involving, you create a cognitive exchange that stimulates and engages the brain. As you carefully navigate when to assert what you know, when to engage the group as equals, and when to let go entirely, and allow learners to discover what they may, learning flourishes. Such an approach to teaching is one that holds attention and drives knowledge acquisition at a more rapid rate than traditional "telling" styles. It engenders confidence and ownership in learners. Varied forms of influence are critical to empowerment and will be covered in greater detail as the chapter unfolds.

Listening for Understanding

The next element of empowering intent is listening for understanding. Primed with a thirst for knowledge, those who empower also wish to know about those around them. In effect, they are well-disposed *active listeners* and typically possess better-than-average *emotional intelligence*. Referenced earlier in the book, these two proclivities are rooted in one's intuitive orientation and carry through to each key IDEA-based trait. They are fundamental to our intuitive orientation as they enable us to attune more accurately and completely. With respect to one's directive force, there is an overarching imperative for empathy-guided drive. Now when we act from empowering intent, the need to listen for understanding is essential. It helps to ensure that others will be able to achieve what we are sanctioning them to do.

For me personally, leadership is synonymous with empowerment. I see it as the primary obligation of a leader to recognize and nurture qualities in others that will take them to the next level. I believe what the literature tells us, that getting others to share in the creation of their responsibility is the best way to grow individuals and organizations. When I first took on leadership roles, I was excited to help those around me do more. My assumption was that everyone readily welcomed the chance to have more responsibility. I also thought everyone welcomed the opportunity to be coached on how to get there. What can I tell you? I was very young and hopelessly idealistic. When someone balked, I chalked it up to humbleness or to minor jitters. I thought if I just nudged them, they would get over it. When someone tried to push past me, I thought they were overly enthusiastic. I played down the trepidations of some and the egos of others and believed they would all eventually settle in.

The fact of the matter was I needed to listen better in order to lead better. The more leadership roles I took on, the more I learned how critical it was to listen, to really pay attention to what was going on around me. I had to resist my own urge to forge forward, and learn to regularly step back and recap what was happening. Prior to this epiphany, I instead acted like the proverbial mommy bird prodding the baby birds out of the nest. Mine were the best of intentions, but I had a fatal leadership flaw. I was treating everyone the same. I wasn't tuned in to individual differences, to the range of proclivities of those on my teams. What I eventually came to discover was a sort of empowerment-receptivity continuum. I had some zealous little birds ready to fly out of the nest at Mach speed. Some of these little ones often ploughed forward so that they left a mess in their wake. They wanted as much responsibility as possible with little or no parameters. I came to realize that this personality type was oblivious to its negative impacts. These people also seem to lack awareness of their own limitations. Many of them could be coached to align better, tone down their drive, and play better in the sandbox, so to speak. They ultimately recalibrated well and became key contributors. Some, though, were more ingrained in their resistance, closed off to feedback, and ultimately they crashed and burned.

Those at the other extreme, those with hesitancies, needed help building confidence and independence. They were coachable, requiring different forms of support. Once they got the attention they needed, most did very well. It was leadership time well spent as many were now more vital and resilient.

Still others fell more into the middle of the continuum and simply required fine tuning of one type or another. They too did fine.

All in all, it served as a great exercise in the higher-level nuances of leadership listening. I learned that in order to empower others you have to know them very well, meet them where they are, and adjust your "teaching" to address a full range of possibilities. The very good news about listening as an aspect of empowerment is that once you are wired to react that way, you will attune better to all aspects of your leadership. You will naturally understand the customer, the competition, and the challenges you face better. You are more apt to navigate the business landscape better and respond with greater facility to change and crisis.

In closing this section on empowerment, I'd like to share another "little birds in the nest" story, this one conveyed through the words to a song.

> *A scared baby wren, perched high on a shelf*
> *The nest was empty except for herself*
> *The others had flown, they were stronger than she.*
> *She crept to the edge, for an hour looked at me.*
> *Sensing I'd do no harm, she flew and landed on my arm*
> *A rare and beautiful surprise*
> *An ancient wisdom in her eyes, her courage seemed to say*
> *Face your fears or be alone,*
> *And then she flew away.*[4]

Friend, song-writer, and retired business woman Denise Cantrell wrote the above piece. Her lyrics connect us to the essence of empowering intent. Denise was inspired to write this song when she read a story in a popular magazine about an aspiring artist who had a family of wrens nesting in the rafters of his studio. All of the birds left the nest except for one. The artist saw the reticent wren as a sign giving him the courage to pursue art as his life's work. If the reluctant wren could take this leap onto his arm, he must take a leap of his own. The artist gave permission to Denise to make the story into a song.

Collective Orientation

Once the proper level-setting has occurred and coaching issues have been addressed, you are now positioned to let your birds fly freely and safely. Done properly, individuals are well prepared, comfortable with their responsibility, and clear about their accountabilities. They can and should continue to turn to you for support along the way. The leader's interest continues to be focused on seeing to it that each and every member becomes empowered to the mutual benefit of the group. As individuals work to make their unique contributions, they do so as members of a team. Diversity is brought to bear, and outcomes are enriched. You can now take a well-earned, relaxing deep breath as members come into their own. Your role now turns to one of stewardship, mentoring, and encouragement. The leader sees to it that a continued sharing between and among group members naturally occurs and a powerful cooperative unfolds. By driving a culture whereby others organically share their greater knowledge, the team is on its way to a sustainable method of operating.

SILOES: THE ULTIMATE ENERGY DRAIN

What happens when the opposite is the case—when you don't push for a collective state, but instead allow individuals and departments to work in siloes? Goals can still be met and individuals can still excel, but a vast amount of energy is wasted. Each separate member or division functions in its silo without the benefit of full team support. Strength is also sapped as separate people and factions do things "their way" without a real sense for the issues or limitations of peer groups. Leaders are then blindsided when reality hits and one group cannot deliver what another one needs in order to function. Major screw-ups occur because you have internal groups competing with each other. Someone has to suffer as a result.

The fact is that many organizations still function this way. Such cultures push leaders to commit to unrealistic goals and push their respective parties to do their discrete parts. Little time is spent listening to the issues, and even less time is devoted to building communication and accountabilities as a team. What tends to occur is people work harder and harder but hit the proverbial walls with nowhere to turn for assistance. Workers feel disempowered even when given more rein because they cannot accomplish what is expected of them no matter how capable they are. Worse yet, peer groups are forced to compete rather than work together. Compliance may seem to exist on the surface. Folks persevere and do the best that they can, but they avoid responsibility when they have room to. Finger-pointing is rampant as no one is really sure who is to blame because they are not working together in the first place.

Those with the power to address this cultural conundrum need to see the business opportunity in cultivating high-functioning collaborative teams over the far less desirable practice of driving individuals to the breaking point.

BUILT TO ENDURE

The true differentiator of empowering leadership approaches is the sustainability factor. Gains are realized and repeated into the future. People in organizations can leave (even key people), and things don't fall apart. Folks can move to another division or group and easily assimilate in. Can you think of a situation in your life, whether at home, at work, or elsewhere, where major effort and energy is expended without sustainable results? How about when you have to tell your child for the hundredth time to do something, or having to start back at square one at work following a restructuring event? Have you travelled anywhere lately that involves flying with a major air carrier and experienced a frustration? These are all examples of deficiencies in sustainability. Tasks, even seemingly simple ones, can't seem to be done well with efficiency. When you lead with empowering intent, you focus on the acquisition of repeatable results. Ownership and accountability as hallmarks of empowerment are carried forward to produce systems and processes that get it right and keep it that way. A conduit is in place that automatically conveys continuous improvement opportunities through a diverse exchange of inputs from all involved. Members interact with each other with commitment and concern.

Because most of us travel by plane at one time or another and many do so regularly, let's look to the airlines to illustrate some key points. While commercial airlines must retain most of the control for everyone's safety, there is still, believe it or not, a small and potent place for empowerment in the flight process that would not only make the experience more pleasant but more effective as well. All it would take would be minor attention to emotional intelligence and active listening, and a small but important facet of ownership given to passengers. Are you intrigued? I actually experienced it in part just a few weeks ago with an empowering flight attendant. His approach will be described in a moment. First, let's look at how the airline could get us ready to be on board (pun intended) in advance.

It would start with a few easy-to-digest statements on your ticket when you purchase it. Not pages and pages of fine-print legalese but rather five or so statements in prominent print that clearly spell out what the passenger can expect from the airline and what the airline expects from us. The last statement can also refer to the remaining fine print, but by engaging people in something they are more likely to read and understand, we start the process off better. It says, "We are in this together. This is what we will do, and this is what we need from you regarding your luggage and how to best board the aircraft." When you get to the gate, cordial announcements regarding boarding would occur rather than an uptight recitation of policy. The more civil the tone, the more engaged most passengers would be. Now we get to the flight attendant who related to passengers with empowering style.

This particular gentleman was a seasoned employee who seemed to quite like his job. As we boarded the aircraft, he moved about the cabin busily and positively. He came across as someone totally invested in the process. He came on the microphone asking everyone to get seated. He spoke respectfully and conversationally. When he arrived at the point in his duties where he needed to ask for electronic devices to be turned off, he made an upbeat but direct plea that worked well. He said, "Hi everyone, listen, we need you to turn off all electronic devices, and believe me, we absolutely know how hard it is for you to do this, but you have to do it now so we can get going. Thanks so much." Everyone chuckled. I looked around and, to a person, everyone shut off and stowed their laptops, phones, and tablets. Folks were smiling and chuckling in agreement. This may seem like a trivial and even absurd example, but it demonstrates how active listening as a function of empowerment works. The attendant was speaking from a place of understanding. We responded in kind. He gave similar instructions about getting seated and stowing carry-on bags, and things went quite smoothly. People were actually helping and policing each other in a supportive manner. Compared to what I've typically experienced during this same process on other flights, it was fairly striking. When we think about leaders applying some of these simple principles to the nature of their dialogues, the possibilities would be significant.

Another way to think about why this flight attendant was so successful in gaining compliance is through the perspective of Malcolm Knowles, a leading theorist in adult learning. Knowles believed in what he termed *andragony*, a method of helping adults take on responsibility for their learning, thus becoming more empowered. To clarify, the word is spelled properly. Knowles' *andragony* is different from the word *androgyny* described earlier in the book as someone with masculine and feminine style traits. Knowles's andragony is

ON EMPOWERMENT AND POWER

When we think of empowerment, we mistakenly see it as a soft skill. It is anything but. It is actually nurturing-based, but not in the flowery sense of the word—rather as in the most potent form of energy. Think of empowerment as Margaret Fuller represents knowledge: something we possess that we share in order to enable. Empowering intent assumes power as something to engender in order to create something greater still. It is far from the masculine-based notion of power as something one seeks to attain, hold onto, and build for one's self. As such it reflects a collective leadership position where benefits grow exponentially for all involved, not just for those at the positional head.

based on the premise that adults are more apt to seek learning that they can incorporate into their experiences and thus apply to what they are expected to do. Knowles sees teaching and leading more as mentoring and assumes that adults willingly seek out what is relevant to them.[5] This flight attendant related to passengers as an empathic mentor and, as such, brought relevancy to bear.

WHY WOMEN ARE NATURALS

In 2007, McKinsey and Company, in partnership with the Women's Forum for the Economy and Society, published *Women Matter: Gender Diversity, a Corporate Performance Driver.* Their report showed a correlation between the proportion of women in management and the companies' performance. The report argued that gender diversity was crucial not simply as a social concern but because having more women in management positions was better for the viability of the business. The report further noted that the nature of emerging global challenges further necessitated a gender-integrated leadership platform.

This year, the McKinsey Women's Forum partnership conducted a follow-up study in which 1,000 managers of varied companies were studied. The study, called Women Matter 2, found women to score higher on five of nine specific leadership behaviors directly tied to business performance today. On two additional behaviors men and women scored the same, and on the remaining two behaviors men scored higher. If we examine more specifically the nine behaviors themselves, we see something fascinating relative to the behaviors and the components of empowerment. The five behaviors women scored significantly higher on were people development, expectations and rewards, role modelling, inspiration, and participative decision-making. Intellectual stimulation and efficient communication were the two behaviors women and men scored equally on. If we map the components of empowerment directly to these seven behaviors, we see that empowerment requires teaching, coaching, and mentoring (intellectual stimulation, role modelling, and efficient communication). Empowerment also consists of listening and the ability to assess individuals and teams (people development). Empowerment is other- rather than self-focused, whereby individuals are prompted to excel and reap the benefits of their success (expectation and rewards and inspiration). Finally, empowerment seeks to internalize and broaden developmental impact through a collective and inclusive positioning (participative decision-making).

The two behaviors men scored higher on were individual decision-making and control and corrective action. These two behaviors tie directly to an individualistic form of power. While they have a necessary place in a leader's skill set, when employed without empowering abilities, they leave leaders and their teams coming up short. Women Matter 2 made the additional point that in order to reap the benefits of the full range of leadership behaviors required to meet today's complex business challenges, we need a gender-assimilated leadership team where women reach equal or better positional levels. Women reaching critical mass on the leadership team is necessary in order for their different leadership perspectives to be actualized within the group.[6] This study lends credence to the vital place of empowerment in leadership. It seems no longer positioned as a "nice to have" style but rather an essential "must have" leadership trait.

Empowerment and Maternal Attachment: A Developmental Imperative

Women are naturally disposed to empower. It is at the very core of who we are and stems from our own maternal attachment. Maternal attachment is a developmental process first described by John Bowlby whereby the infant forms a bond with his or her primary caregiver, typically the baby's mother. Bowlby believed that attachment was biologically driven for both mother and infant, meaning it was part of an evolutionary process whereby both saw it as a matter of survival. For vulnerable infants to survive, they had to be close to their mother, who would care for and protect them. The completely dependent infant innately seeks out its caregiver. Moreover, Bowlby postulated that the nature of the caregiver's responses to the infant shaped the future development of the child. Bowlby described a securely attached child as one whose maternal figure was responsive to his or her needs. The child whose attachment was a solid one grew with a stable foundation and approached the world in an assured and steady manner. If, on the other hand, the caregiver was unresponsive or inconsistent, the child grew with a more anxious orientation. The child's foundation was erratic and unpredictable, and it made navigating life more tenuous. Depending on the child's continued life circumstances and the child's own personal resilience, behavioral issues would or could manifest.[7]

A second developmental theorist, Donald Winnicott, described attachment in terms of a *holding environment* created by the mother, who learns from her mother how to care for, protect, and support her baby. Winnicott more precisely described the holding environment as interactions between mother and child whereby the mother supports the child when and how deemed necessary for the well-being and safety of the child. Actual holding, comfort, and touch are very much a part of the facilitative world the mother attempts to create. The better the holding environment, the more secure the attachment. The more secure the attachment, the more comfortable the child is as he or she grows toward independence.

A crucial facet of the holding environment is how the mother loosens it as the child shows capability. Direction and prompting may be provided by the mother as she prods the young one to more and more autonomy. The adequate holding environment makes it clear to learners what is expected of them and how much control and influence you intend to exert over the process. Being warm and supportive does help the learners assume their rightful place in the scheme. The construct of the holding environment is how women learned to empower, whether as a mother to a child, a teacher to students, or a leader to direct reports.

The second aspect of Winnicott's holding environment is his concept of the good-enough mother. The *good-enough mother* is a well-intending but fallible figure, exposing those in her care to the realities of an imperfect world, helping them to reconcile frustration and cope with their own unmet needs. The good-enough mother role helps prepare children for the normal frustrations and disappointments they will encounter in life. As such, the mother need not be a perfect caregiver but one who does the best she can to raise her baby.[8] Through the attachment theories of Bowlby and Winnicott, we begin to see how women are socioculturally cast to be empowering leaders and where feminine perspectives on learning and empowerment originated.

Women know and live ways of attachment, holding environments, and the good-enough mother role. These development constructs form the basis of their interpersonal dealings in leadership and life. We tend to see the overall success of the business as directly correlated with successful empowerment. Whether you have had children of your own or have shared naturally in the development of those close to you, most women are drawn to facilitate success in others. As such, women are hard-wired to empower, to care for, and to support. With thousands of years of womanhood to draw from, we have all been for someone the *good-enough mother*. Our empowerment die has been firmly cast. We live it, we get it, and we treasure it. It is, therefore, only natural that when most women get into the leadership arena, their tendency is to include others, to feel a responsibility for those around them, and to share power. We naturally view work as a collective, a team. Empowerment is our deeply rooted priority.

What about the empowering intent of women who have not actually had children of their own? Does it matter? Speaking from personal knowledge and experience, there seems to be a fairly substantial number of professional women who don't have children for one reason or another and remain empowering by nature. I know this because I am one of them, as are a number of my friends and colleagues. We either couldn't have children due to health reasons, life circumstances being such that the opportunity didn't present itself, or because some choose not to. Most of the women I know who have not had children of their own have pets that they raise as one would raise a child. In my case I have two Westies, Max and Lilly. Many who know me say they wish they had the childhood that my dogs have. Many of us also have individuals in their lives that we closely support and mentor, such as nieces and nephews, stepchildren, or the children of friends and relatives. Most in my circle at least relate to our work teams with the same empowering intent that our colleagues with children do. We seem to be drawing on an innate attachment calling. We are drawn to create holding environments and to act as the good-enough mother in the different venues of our lives.

More Compelling Data

In Chapter 2, a research study by Greenberg and Sweeney was introduced citing several personality and motivational strengths that women possess that are instrumental in meeting the leadership challenges of today. Additional results from that study apply to the discussion of women and empowerment. The Greenberg and Sweeney study echoed the findings of the McKinsey/Women's Forum partnership relative to women's strong suits in participatory decision-making. Specifically, Greenberg and Sweeney found women to be more likely to operate from a style of inclusion and team orientation with respect to problem solving and decision-making. Women seemed sincerely committed to hearing all points of view. The ultimate decisions of the women studied seemed to reflect the best of what was heard. They did not thwart others in favor of their original position. Such decision-making is described by Greenberg and Sweeney as informed and as a result of honed listening abilities. It was also found that women leaders shared information more readily and opened lines of dialogue around key issues.[9]

It would stand to reason that if you were born from a competitive social position, you would naturally see power as an individually based means to an end, something that affords you the advantage, something to hold onto in order to help you succeed. This is the masculine perspective. It is reasoned here that seemingly most men (and some women) lead from this power platform. This traditionally masculine perspective is counter to empowerment. If on the other hand you were socialized to attach, to respond, and to include, you would see power as something to share and to propagate in others. Your inclination would be to impart knowledge, to act as an advisor, to hear others out, and to incorporate. Yours would be the perspective that the whole is truly greater because of the collective sum of its parts. This is the feminine perspective. It is thought here that most women and some men lead from this perspective.

THE POWER OF THE COLLECTIVE

Imbedded in the nature of empowerment is a collective orientation. Because the empowering leader's premise is to promote others and to share power, her or his lens is very much a team-based one. From such a perspective it would be difficult if not impossible to empower discretely. You instead look to connect those you empower to share knowledge and drive a greater whole. Today's world works through collectives. Social networking is a prime example. Another is how global businesses are now structured through intricate and virtual matrixes. A collective orientation is what enables structures such as these to thrive. Territorialism is the enemy as it undermines interconnectedness.

In addition to being other- and group-centered, empowering individuals have an appreciation for diversity. They tend to see differences as interesting and enriching. Group dynamics is the study of how collectives function. The impact of diversity is a key element in group dynamics research. According to the group dynamics literature, the most impactful groups are those with diversity in perspective. A diverse group is termed a heterogeneous one. As the name implies, a heterogeneous group is composed of members who are different from each other. Heterogeneous groups, though initially more difficult to manage, net greater innovation and resilience. They require more complex communication skills between and among members, but they also are capable of producing more enriched outcomes. Overall, heterogeneous groups that function well come to see discovery and learning as means to a more enhanced end.

A homogeneous group, on the other hand, is one that is composed of members who are very much alike. They can be similar in age, gender, beliefs, ethnicity, or religious backgrounds. There are multiple common threads that connect members to each other. The more homogeneous a group, the more easily members get along and the more quickly they come to decisions. Yet it is also noted that homogeneous groups tend to be more limited in their thinking. While seemingly easier to manage or work within, there is only so much like-membered groups can accomplish. They have a limited pool of information to consider and are constricted in terms of cognitive range. Because they are constrained in their knowledge base, they can be closed off to learning anything outside of their specific view.

A highly functioning group, then, is one that is varied in composition and has the skills necessary to navigate and therefore leverage its assortment. These groups tend to thrive on shared conscientiousness. Each person feels that he or she has a voice in the collective and a unique contribution to make. Said in the language of Winnicott, the group is run through an optimum holding environment, one that gives the level of support needed while allowing (and expecting) individual autonomy to flourish so long as contributions are shared and are for the good of the whole.

High-functioning groups seem the future of successful businesses. In order to effectively hone and execute a uniquely strategic value proposition, a team would have to share knowledge, leverage diversity, and communicate openly, directly, and clearly. As operating costs continue to rise and profit margins shrink, everyone will have to execute flawlessly. Trust and motivation will need to be restored in the context of harsh economic realities. Our best chance for doing well in such an environment is through leaders who promote knowledge sharing and who engage others to do more than their part, and through teams with broad skills sets, functionally and interpersonally. This is the platform of empowerment. How, then, does one become more empowering?

THE ART OF EMPOWERING

The foundational skill needed to empower others is active listening. Active listening was described in detail in Chapter 2 as fundamental to intuition and referenced again in Chapter 3 to help establish empathic purpose. Carrying forward and extending from that basis, active listening is your starting point with respect to empowering others. You need well-honed listening skills in order to assess an individual's readiness and shepherd them as they develop through to full ownership, collaboration, and mastery. The additional attributes needed for empowerment center around higher-order influencing and communication skills. These abilities are necessary in order to foster learning cultures and promote the development of high-functioning, diverse teams. Spheres of influence were noted earlier in the chapter. Specific influencing skills will now be presented in detail as they relate to shared versus individual power.

Shared Power and Influence

In the late 1950s, social psychologists John French and Bertram Raven developed a way to look at power as a vehicle for influencing others. Their *six bases of power* represent a widely recognized model in the group dynamics and organizational development literatures. There is great applicability for how one can be more effective at shared power through the use of French and Raven's complete power spectrum. Their basic premise is that power exists in a relationship and, based on the nature of that relationship, one or more of their bases of power will be most effective in helping you to sway others. If we think of empowerment as shared power, leveraging French and Raven's full range of powers will help you to teach, align, motivate, and engender. The six bases of power include are listed in the sidebar.

- Reward power—the ability to provide something that others value
- Coercive power—the ability to set limits or to reprimand
- Legitimate power—authority by virtue of one's position
- Persuasive power—possessing and using information to convince
- Referent power—influence derived from being admired both because others look up to you and because of how you make them feel about themselves
- Expert power—possessing specific skills, knowledge, or expertise[10]

Looking over these six bases of power, which ones do you more naturally exercise when you are trying to get others to take on more responsibility? Which would you be more apt to leverage in order to impart knowledge? What we find is that individuals are more disposed to certain bases of power than to others. The specific bases of power an individual gravitates toward reflect one's interpersonal preferences as well as one's power orientation. People who lead from individual power tend to exercise reward, coercive, and legitimate powers most often to the exclusion of the other three. When it comes to empowerment, though, where shared power is garnered, leaders learn to more readily draw on all six bases of power in the course of their empowering relationships. Doing so creates and maintains a potent holding environment through which individual and team development is nurtured.

Building up to using the complete power continuum takes practice. Use a log and a journal to keep track of your progress. A *log* is a structured, quantitative tool in which you create a chart and record when you've used each form of power. Make entries daily for a period of four weeks by tracking which bases of power you are using. Look over your log weekly using a *journal* to reflect on anything you notice about what you did and why. A journal is less structured and more free flowing than a log. In the first two weeks, note patterns and trends. During weeks three and four, begin to capture thoughts on how you could have incorporated other bases of power into your repertoire in order to get better results. At the end of the four weeks, you should be able to see your power preferences. From there, begin to push yourself to broaden your power applications. Add more and more forms of influence until you are comfortable integrating all six into your leadership approaches. Give yourself four additional weeks to accomplish this.

Once you are comfortable using all six bases of power, concentrate your efforts on how to specifically use the continuum in a given empowering relationship. Pick an individual you wish to develop, someone you see as ready for greater responsibility. Create a plan for what you need to do to prepare the individual (what knowledge they need or what parameters have to be set). Listen carefully and assess how willing they are to take on more. Think of the bases of power best suited to assist you in helping them learn what they need. Once they are comfortable with their new tasks, consider what you now need to do to help guide and encourage them. What bases of power will best support them? The key is that you act from sound influencing strategy. Thoughtfully use the bases of power as they are best suited to this individual's developmental situation. Your focus is on the person in essence becoming more powerful through your conscious application of your power.

Creating a Culture of Learning

What is a culture of learning? It is an environment that places high value on the act of knowing. It is an environment that supports the sharing of information broadly in order to get to best practices. It is a milieu that openly discusses successes and failures and their related impacts and one that seeks to continuously improve. It is not an environment that promotes the personal agendas of those in power or one that focuses exclusively on reaching goals. It is a work setting where teams are valued, individual opinions are heard, and diversity is cultivated. When you foster the belief that knowing is valued as much as accomplishment is, you have established a culture of learning. The decided advantage of such a milieu is that the pooling of resources and strong suits across the organization is possible. Processes and systems are able to be streamlined and redundancy eliminated. Beginning approximately a decade ago, studies showed that companies that paid attention to learning outperformed those that didn't. What does it mean to pay attention to learning? Learning practices become internalized to one's leadership, not remaining solely a function of human resources or training departments. Learning is a continuous formal and informal part of everyday work conversations.

Five approaches are noted in the literature as promoting a learning culture:

1. There must be an *open demonstration* on the part of the leader that she does in fact value learning; show that you are hooked on it—that it is integral to your everyday life. Today's Internet age makes this easier than ever because we have instant access to vast stores of knowledge as well as vehicles to readily share that knowledge.

2. *Provide structured opportunities for groups and teams to convene* and discuss what they know, what they are struggling with, and what they believe they still have to grapple with. Empower teams to come up with ways to get the information they need.

3. *Stick to it.* This cannot be viewed as some new leadership whim or phase. Show commitment and imbed it through inclusion in existing systems and structures.

4. Create embraceable *mantras* regarding learning and weave learning language into the fabric of everyday dialogue.

5. Finally, tell stories. *Storytelling* is a potent form of learning and empowerment. When we tell our stories and receive validation for accomplishments or support for failures, it cements our place as a regarded member. It builds confidence and makes us more likely to take calculated risks, to innovate, and to stretch ourselves further.[11]

Women naturally create learning cultures as they raise their children. One need only observe a group of young mothers comparing stories, learning from each other, and talking about what went right and what they will never ever do again to see evidence of this. It is how women grow as secure caretakers. As women come together and learn from each other about their children, it is clear that this is not the time to compete. Something that is as precious to them as their children makes women readily willing to share knowledge. There is, then, direct carryover from this caretaking practice to how women lead. They naturally see shared knowledge as a potent means to an end. Shared knowledge equates in a woman's mind to shared power. Both become constructs they trust, stand behind, and cherish. Personal power pales in comparison.

Many who study learning cultures find a direct tie-in to innovation; groups that are more open to learning are more innovative. That doesn't seem surprising. If you develop a thirst for information along with a quest for meaning, it would seem likely to propel you into "what's next" action. If you want an entertaining example of a thirst for knowledge and quest for meaning in action, watch the popular U.S. sitcom *The Big Bang Theory*. It's about a group of four brilliant, quirky university researchers who are consumed with learning. While tied by their vocations, they are the epitome of a heterogeneous group. With their scholarly brains in overdrive, it seems there isn't anything they can't decipher, create, and decide. They can never know enough or discover enough, and as a result, an innovative frenzy regularly ensues. While their depiction is comedic hyperbole, it conveys how learning can be infectious as well as a fundamental driver of the inventive. How can you get your own workgroups electrified about learning for extraordinary "big bang" results of your own?

Individual and Team Development

How can you best drive both the individual development of others and the development of teams? Begin by establishing yourself as a *grounded leader*. You must be seen as someone who is consistent, stable, and trustworthy.

Others must feel that they are in good hands. A *grounded leader* is composed (able to control emotions), approachable (having a manner that helps others reach out to you), sincere, pragmatic, rightly cautious, loyal, and proven. In other words, in order to develop individuals and teams, you must first demonstrate the kind of character that others feel safe with. You must be someone they hold in high regard. In French and Bertram's language, you must hold genuine referent power, not simply as a charismatic leader but as a trusted steward.

Next, take a sincere interest in *knowing your people and your teams*. Understand who they are and how they function relative to what you expect of them. See their development as a responsibility shared between you and them. To do this well from your end, begin by building a solid *development network*. Such a network would include people in your organization and in your extended professional sphere with whom you can discuss development experiences and tools. Create regular discussion opportunities with your network regarding talent development. Keep development at the top of your mind. Ensure that you are versed in the most current options out there.

Lastly, hone your ability to *give and receive feedback* so that you can effectively communicate what individuals are doing well and how they need to improve. Feedback was mentioned in Chapter 2 relative to facilitating self-awareness—how you can seek out and interpret feedback from others for your own development. Here you need to become the adept feedback provider. Being able to give adequate feedback takes practice. It is easier for some than others. Think of it as a conversation, not a confrontation. It need not be harsh, only clear, helpful, and genuine. People shouldn't leave a feedback conversation with you having to read between the lines or decipher what you meant. Feedback can and should be a mix of validations and constructive observations. Most people appreciate feedback when it comes from someone they trust. It is especially well received when others know you have their best interest at heart. Giving positive feedback is a great place to start. Then slowly work your way up to more candor about issues or opportunities for improvement. Feedback can also be provided with the premise that you and the recipient will work together on a solution. I often ask the person to tell me how I can help or what they need from me in order to tackle the issue or come up to speed.

Most of what has been described in this section applies to developing individuals and teams alike. In moving deeper and more specifically into additional aspects of team development, it is important to establish and communicate foundational expectations for how you want the team to optimally function. Provide a short team vision, mission, and values platform—how you want the group to function. This is especially important because everyone then gets the same message. Next, empower the group to devise how they will get there and what will be their rules of engagement. Select a good team model to follow. There are several widely held paradigms for high-functioning teams to choose from. Look for one that best aligns with your current context and organizational culture. Require that the team adopt one and follow it. Seek outside facilitative help in understanding individual style preferences, communication dynamics, and conflict approaches. Gain assistance drilling down to the nature of the team's diversity and how to best leverage your team's collective strong suits. Finally, celebrate the successes of individuals and teams publicly and together. Especially call attention to how members are following the established vision, mission, and values. Call out how the team is developing a sound learning culture. Celebrate the courage it takes to share the stories of vulnerabilities. Validate stories of accomplishments.

To review, becoming more empowering begins with building your bases of power so that you grow into a leader with broad-based influencing skills. Becoming more empowering also means that you promote the sharing of knowledge and see learning as the means to innovation and success. Next, look to your character and ask yourself, "Am I the kind of leader others can trust?" "Am I a good steward; someone others feel compelled to be empowered by?" Finally, see it as your central leadership task to direct the development of the individuals and groups within your charge. Invest in others, and they will respond in kind. Let's look now at those individuals who are in fact exemplars of empowering intent.

EMPOWERMENT EXEMPLARS

In thinking about empowerment exemplars, one would first give credit to womanhood as a group and a culture. Over time and across the globe, women everywhere have been pioneers and advocates of empowerment. They are natural role models of it. Each and every woman presented in the book so far should therefore be re-recognized as well for their ability to empower. It is an innate ability for women to nurture those whose lives they touch. I would like to share a story of a colleague in order to drive this point home. Her husband recently lost his job. The company he was employed with for 15 years dissolved, and everyone lost their jobs without severance compensation. Fortunately, he found another job, though one that would relocate the family across the country. My colleague is a district manager of a sales team, and she will be able to continue her work from their new location. As we discussed the move, I found what she revealed to be both moving and affirming with respect to the topic at hand.

She is a remarkable mom, a consummate professional, and an all-around delightful person. I came over one day to find her struggling with their pending relocation. Through her tears she expressed that although her children were now in college and therefore not being uprooted, she and the kids were devastated because the children's lifelong friends would no longer be able to call their home a second home. She relayed quite plainly and naturally that these dozen-plus kids were in affect her kids too; she had been a part of their lives for more than 10 years. She watched them grow to young adulthood. She helped them through rough spots and shared in their successes as they ate meals with her, socialized, and shared their lives together. She relayed how each one had come over with a gift of thanks for all she had done for them. One boy in particular gave her a batch of cookies he baked himself. They were the very same cookies (his favorite) that she had baked for him all these years.

Listening to her speak, you could feel the empowerment process of a woman that extended into the lives of these children. Whether the friends of one's own children, one's neighbor's children, or one's extended family members, women reach out and involve themselves directly in the development of others. Woman like my friend approach life through the lens of empowerment.

For an example of an empowering woman familiar to all of us, we can look to the current first lady of the United States, Michelle Obama. First Lady Obama is the quintessential example of an empowering woman. Michelle Robinson Obama came from humble beginnings. She is often heard describing her family life as loving, happy, and genuine. Her parents worked hard to provide for her and for her brother. Her father, in particular, faced tremendous adversity, being stricken with a degenerative disease, yet he persevered without complaint, determined to provide for his family. A gifted student, Michelle went on to earn advanced degrees at prestigious schools. She practiced law at a Chicago firm, which is where she met her husband, Barack. Two years later they were married. Michelle also worked in high-profile community-service positions for the city of Chicago and for the University of Chicago and its hospital system. We came to know her when she embarked with presidential candidate Obama on their road to the White House.

The couple became parents first in 1999 when daughter Malia was born and again in 2001 with the birth of their second daughter, Sasha. The first lady is often heard referring to herself as "Mom in Chief" as her family is her first priority. Important to note are the causes she has focused on as first lady. You will clearly see a nurturing emphasis throughout them. Her efforts include working with Second Lady Dr. Jill Biden to support military families, helping women better address the challenges of work/life balance, encouraging national service and volunteerism in others, the development of education, and finally helping everyone, children especially, to be more health and wellness conscious, to exercise and eat right.[12]

If you observe the first lady and listen to her speak, you see and hear repeated examples of her broad-based influencing skill. She leverages all bases of power naturally: her *legitimate* authority, *persuasive* knowledge base, *referent* charm, and *expertise*, to name a few. Each form of influence comes through in her actions, speaking, and causes. You have even heard the president himself lovingly joke about her firm limit-setting with him and their daughters (her *coercive* power).

This section about the first lady is being written two days after her address at the 2012 Democratic Convention. In that speech the first lady repeatedly stressed the power of the collective—how we must work together and grow together. Here is an excerpt from that speech in which the first lady conveys her and the president's values and foundational beliefs as taught by their families and passed onto them—values and beliefs that underscore a collective orientation:

> We learned about dignity and decency—that how hard you work matters more than how much you make . . . that helping others means more than just getting ahead yourself. We learned about honesty and integrity—that the truth matters . . . that you don't take shortcuts or play by your own set of rules . . . and success doesn't count unless you earn it fair and square. We learned about gratitude and humility—that so many people had a hand in our success, from the teachers who inspired us to the janitors who kept our school clean . . . and we were taught to value everyone's contribution and treat everyone with respect. Those are the values Barack and I—and so many of you—are trying to pass on to our own children. . . . that when you've worked hard, and done well, and walked through that doorway of opportunity . . . you do not slam it shut behind you . . . you reach back, and you give other folks the same chances that helped you succeed. Because today, I know from experience that if I truly want to leave a better world for my daughters, and all our sons and daughters . . . if we want to give all our children a foundation for their dreams and opportunities worthy of their promise . . . if we want to give them that sense of limitless possibility—that belief that here in America, there is always something better out there if you're willing to work for it . . . then we must work like never before . . . and we must once again come together and stand together. . . .[13]

Michelle Obama lives her life from the premise that one's individual success and accomplishment is a vehicle for helping others to be more and to achieve more. She also believes that it is her personal responsibility to leave the world better than she found it by identifying where others are developing, struggling, or headed down the wrong path and helping to support or redirect them. She sees all that she is as being for the benefit of others. Most importantly, she seems not to act as she does simply because she is a good person but because she believes in empowerment as a means for humanity to thrive; she believes that the more positively connected we are to each other, the greater the overall outcomes. She sees that as you give back and join people to one another, diversity is potentiated. She is the veritable empowering woman. She exemplifies the empowering spirit.

While she is a tough act to follow, many other accomplished women (and men) operate from the first lady's perspective. In order to be as proficient at empowerment as she is, though, one would have to rate highly on each of the following qualities:

- You are more focused on helping others than on getting ahead.
- You are warm, caring, and passionate.
- You are trustworthy and looked up to.
- You believe in the power of knowledge.
- You are an avid learner, and you listen in order to understand.
- You promote the sharing of knowledge between and among others.
- You are inclusive.
- You are likely to take charge for the sake of bringing others up to speed rather than to control things yourself.
- You are drawn to diversity and novelty.
- You believe that progress best occurs when we work collectively.

Where do you fall on this scale? Who do you know who you would rate as empowering as Michelle Obama?

COMING TOGETHER

From empowering intent we move to the final IDEA-based leadership trait. We proceed from empowering others to assimilating, or bringing others together not just to collaborate but to better coexist. Through an assimilative nature we learn how to more deeply understand disparate views. We recognize better where there is common ground (what binds us) versus where we need to respect each other's uniqueness. We better understand what we can and should expect from each other, and we agree to deliver on that. In the IDEA-based leadership model, we have come to see how insight and foresight (*intuitive orientation*) informs action or *directive force*. We saw how action must translate into *empowering intent* in order to build sustainable capacity. In our final key trait, *assimilative nature*, we see a leadership proclivity that helps establish and effect meaningful bilateral unions.

CHAPTER 5

ASSIMILATIVE NATURE

If we are to achieve a richer culture, rich in contrasting values, we must recognize the whole gamut of human potentialities, and so weave a less arbitrary social fabric, one in which each diverse human gift will find a fitting place.

—Margaret Mead[1]

WHAT IT MEANS TO BE ASSIMILATIVE

The above quote by noted anthropologist Margaret Mead is especially fitting given the state of the world today. The Middle East is exploding with contention both within individual nations and with respect to these nations' strife against the West. Economic and political competitions rage among global superpowers. The 2012 presidential elections in the United States showed polarization like never before and a clearly broken Washington. The ability to face, understand, and address diversity issues seems of paramount importance to whether humankind will move to a more assimilated place or simply self-destruct. The stakes are actually that high. On September 20, 2012, CNN lead Wolf Blitzer interviewed Hina Rabbani Khar, the 26th foreign minister of Pakistan. Rabbani Khar is a Pakistani stateswoman and economist. She became the first female foreign minister of the country in July 2011. She is the highest-ranking female officer in Pakistan's political sphere and is known for her astute diplomacy in forging bilateral relations.

Khar was asked by Blitzer if she believed that the differences between the East and West could ever be resolved. Her reply was a hopeful one. She pointed to the need for both sides to work to truly grasp and accept the fundamental differences between them. Rabbini Khar went on to describe a level of shared insight into each other's values, religious and otherwise, as a crucial determinant in the peace equation.[2] Such are the words and perspectives of an assimilative leader. They also reflect a tenor that is far easier said than done, often glossed over by those whose inclinations are more toward winning than coming together. Assimilation represents a progressive view, and it is most definitely tedious work, but with far-reaching benefits. To assimilate does not mean that one has to give up power or lose one's individuality. For those who don't readily see value in communal orientations, though, it certainly can feel that way.

Foreign Minister Rabbani Khar was in the United States that week on a four-day visit to meet with U.S. senator John Kerry and the Senate Foreign Relations Committee. Their mission was to begin building a relationship of "mutual respect" between the United States and Pakistan. Tensions between the two countries had mounted over the past year and a half following what was seen by Pakistan as a unilateral counterterrorism action taken by the United States: the discovery and killing of Osama bin Laden inside Pakistan. Also adding to the tension on Pakistan's side was a CIA contractor's killing of two Pakistanis and the accidental killing of 24 Pakistani troops in November by NATO forces. The United States, on the other hand, stresses its need for complete assurances from Pakistan that it will work with the United States on a candid common platform of absolutely halting terrorism. Additionally, the two factions must agree wholeheartedly to work in concert toward a secure Afghanistan, which is clearly in both countries' favor.[3] The trust that needs to be built to work both sides of this particular equation is no small task given the vast differences in cultures. Rabbani Khar encourages us to believe, though, that through mutual understanding it is possible.

Also on September 20, 2012, the *Huffington Post* reported that, according to Rabbani Khar, Pakistan, the United States, and Afghanistan planned to meet formally to begin a dialogue regarding key points of contention among the three countries. To begin with, this group will have to agree on how to deal with the imbedded and al-Qaida-tied, Pakistan-based Haqqani terrorist network. The Haqqani group is considered by Pakistan to be an Afghani refugee faction that the Pakistani military is not yet committed to taking action against, while the United States sees it as a direct impediment to U.S. efforts in Afghanistan.[4] Sorting out how to address the insidious nature of the terrorist webs is one of the many complex aspects this triad will be expected to address.

To be assimilative is to bring people and constructs together. As such, it reflects a cornerstone ability of those who can transform and effect change. Anthropologist Margaret Mead understands this full well. From her knowledge base in the study of the constructs, meanings, and beliefs that bind cultures, she calls attention to the value in learning from each other's views. The intent is not for all to become one but rather that we allow our distinctions to be called out. Doing so allows us, according to Meade, to leverage a prolific assemblage of resources toward the greater good. It also puts us in a better position to coexist in peace through mutual trust, respect, and tolerance.

A MOTHER-TO-CHILD HERITAGE

I was speaking this year at a conference for women. During the presentation, I asked the audience what women could do as individuals to advance the integration of feminine thinking into leadership. One woman stood up and said that as mothers, we can be mindful of the ways we raise our sons and what we teach them from a woman's perspective. The group applauded in resounding agreement. This is a simple yet potent means to change the leadership culture from the bottom up. There is one particular woman whose rearing of her son deserves mention here. That individual is (Stanley) Ann Dunham. Ann Dunham was not a name we would have known until most recently. She is the single mother who raised President Barack Obama.

Ann Dunham was seen by her peers as a forward thinker well beyond her years and time. Her intellect, compassion, and quest for justice set her apart. Hers were not the usual teenage preoccupations. Ann's interests were less about her immediate social collective and more about the issues facing humanity. Her perspective and concerns would eventually take her to a life that transcended typical borders. It is not surprising that such a woman gave rise to a son whose vision was and is to change the world. Ann Dunham is being cited here to call attention to how being truly assimilative works and what it can result in for the good of all concerned. She, like Meade, was an anthropologist by education, so her life was entrenched in cultures and meaning. As such, she was a master at empathy.

Ann Dunham was married twice, once to Barack Obama's father and the second time to an Indonesian man. On a micro scale, Dunham's assimilative nature led her to maintain amicable relationships with both former husbands, a developmental benefit for her two children. A foundational assimilative trait that Dunham displayed in her cordial relationships with these two men was acceptance. One need not agree with, choose to be with, or even like the traits of another, but in order to be assimilative, one must accept the other. Acceptance begets tolerance, and tolerance begets higher-level empathic abilities. Those who excel in empathy have a decided edge in what was earlier described as other-awareness, a skill that then allows them to influence their current circumstances and their greater surroundings.

On a broader level, Dunham's assimilative nature fostered openness to learning, being attuned to her surroundings, and the ability to deal with and adeptly reconcile ambiguity. These were all traits she purposefully taught her son in preparing him for life in a globally engaged world.[5] Whether she knew or not how far her son Barack would take her teachings, the result was that Obama grew to be an unusually facile leader, adept at negotiating complexity and diversity. The president is intricately assimilative, as you will see from the following example. In June 2009, shortly after taking office, President Obama embarked on a groundbreaking tour of the Middle East that culminated in Egypt, where he delivered a 55-minute address at Cairo University. In a worldwide broadcast to 2 billion Muslims throughout the Arab and Muslim world, the president sought to recast the United States' global image and perspective. Critiques of the speech stated that his messages were resoundingly positive. As an example of the praise, the June 5, 2009, edition of *Financial Times* said, "The speech was brilliant. With artful sensitivity he navigated through the minefields littered with cultural explosive devices and politic-religious booby traps, dodging ambushes without evading the issues."[6] CNN senior political analyst David Gergen reported it to be "The most powerful and persuasive speech ever by any American president to the Muslim world."[7] Looking to excerpts from the president's address, we can examine numerous assimilative traits portrayed:

> I am honored to be in the timeless city of Cairo, and to be hosted by two remarkable institutions. For over a thousand years, Al-Azhar has stood as a beacon of Islamic learning, and for over a century, Cairo University has been a source of Egypt's advancement. Together, you represent the harmony between tradition and progress. I am grateful for your hospitality, and the hospitality of the people of Egypt. I am also proud to carry with me the goodwill of the American people, and a greeting of peace from Muslim communities in my country: assalaamu alaykum.[8]

In his brief beginning sentences, Obama demonstrated how he was open to learning as he came into the situation well studied. He let the audience know that he had taken the time to become familiar with them. He demonstrated empathy as he greeted them in their vernacular. As his speech continued, he conveyed more facts and history, setting a context of mutual purpose. Through this knowledge-based skill, the president was able to show that he and those he represents were one entity yet that he fully understood others. Through the power of information, he demonstrated credibility in understanding. In Obama's case, he communicated to the world and to the people before him that he knew full well how we had arrived at the present juncture.

He built trust and respect based on his factually accurate, balanced, and candid story. Obama continued:

> We meet at a time of tension between the United States and Muslims around the world—tension rooted in historical forces that go beyond any current policy debate. The relationship between Islam and the West includes centuries of coexistence and cooperation, but also conflict and religious wars. More recently, tension has been fed by colonialism that denied rights and opportunities to many Muslims, and a Cold War in which Muslim-majority countries were too often treated as proxies without regard to their own aspirations. Moreover, the sweeping change brought by modernity and globalization led many Muslims to view the West as hostile to the traditions of Islam. Violent extremists have exploited these tensions in a small but potent minority of Muslims. The attacks of September 11th, 2001, and the continued efforts of these extremists to engage in violence against civilians have led some in my country to view Islam as inevitably hostile not only to America and Western countries, but also to human rights. This has bred more fear and mistrust. So long as our relationship is defined by our differences, we will empower those who sow hatred rather than peace, and who promote conflict rather than the cooperation that can help all of our people achieve justice and prosperity. This cycle of suspicion and discord must end.[9]

Drawing from an established and unbiased learning foundation, a compelling case for change is more readily able to be considered. An evolution of circumstance was described. Blame was not assigned; instead, factual depictions of a changing world were chronicled. Obama's statements showed a solid historical foundation and an acknowledgement of current realities as well. He comprehensively referenced specific recent conflicts, circumstances, and issues. His presence in Cairo along with the words spoken demonstrated his intent to bring people and cultures together for a common end state. As such, he served as a catalyst of change. In the closing paragraphs of Obama's Cairo address, we saw additional facets of his assimilative ability by his conveying that which was common to all with respect to the religious doctrines of the world.

> All of us share this world for but a brief moment in time. The question is whether we spend that time focused on what pushes us apart, or whether we commit ourselves to an effort—a sustained effort—to find common ground, to focus on the future we seek for our children, and to respect the dignity of all human beings. It is easier to start wars than to end them. It is easier to blame others than to look inward; to see what is different about someone than to find the things we share. But we should choose the right

path, not just the easy path. There is also one rule that lies at the heart of
every religion—that we do unto others as we would have them do unto
us. This truth transcends nations and peoples—a belief that isn't new; that
isn't black or white or brown; that isn't Christian, or Muslim or Jew. It's a
belief that pulsed in the cradle of civilization, and that still beats in the heart
of billions. It's a faith in other people, and it's what brought me here today.
We have the power to make the world we seek, but only if we have the
courage to make a new beginning, keeping in mind what has been written.
The Holy Koran tells us, "O mankind! We have created you male and a
female; and we have made you into nations and tribes so that you may know
one another." The Talmud tells us: "The whole of the Torah is for the
purpose of promoting peace." The Holy Bible tells us, "Blessed are the
peacemakers, for they shall be called sons of God." The people of the world
can live together in peace. We know that is God's vision. Now, that must be
our work here on Earth. Thank you. And May God's peace be with you.[10]

The president's mother-taught assimilative abilities come through in this
noteworthy address and in how he typically approaches interactions. He
makes public statements often about the value of candid and even contentious
discussion, provided both sides are respected. In addition to his assimilative
skill, the president is androgynous in his blending of masculine and feminine
leadership traits, no doubt also the result of his mother's influence. His
evolved leadership approach marks what we can and should aspire toward,
yet the reactions he receives by his opposition, while principally politically
motivated, still show the gap we have in bringing integrated leadership to
the forefront. More germane here, though, is the positive result when mothers
teach feminine leadership strong suits to their sons.

EMPATHY TO THE MAX

The leadership value of empathy was first introduced in Chapter 2 as a
foundational result of one's intuitive orientation. Active listening was one tool
described as a means for developing greater empathy. In Chapter 3, the tie-in
was made to empathy, calling attention to the fact that feminine directive force
originates from empathic purpose—that one has in mind the good of the
group over self-serving drives. Then, in Chapter 4, empathy was noted as central to empowering intent—to being able to be attuned to others in order to
create optimal developmental environments. Empowering intent also
describes a focus on the collective and on using empathy to understand and
leverage each discrete part of the whole. Now we move to the place of empathy
in one's assimilative nature. Think of it as an empathy continuum, building in
skill and complexity as you move through the IDEA model. You begin with

an intuitive nature in which empathy is used to sense the perspectives around you. You grow to apply what you've learned about those around you to accomplish certain goals and tasks in your directive force. From there you involve a full group through empowerment. Now, drawing from an assimilative nature, you now look outside your immediate group to bring together or coexist with external factions.

What, then, does this higher level of empathy entail? I was out to dinner recently with friends. The upcoming presidential election came up. The three couples happened to actually consist of one liberal, one conservative, and one moderate pair. We each began to talk about issues. What ensued was a high-level empathic conversation. It was more classroom-like than like a debate; the speaking tone was mostly low, though it did get passionate at times. The tonal ebb and flow kept the discussion interesting but contained. All three sides asked relevant questions, and in response factual data and personal opinions were expressed but were clearly identified as one or the other. Subjective statements such as, "My personal concern is . . ." or "My own opinion is . . . ," were made on the one hand while in addition facts were called out and declared to be so. The fact-checkers would have been very proud of us as we stuck to substantiated realities. While some things were *very* hard to hear, I left better informed and with some things to think about that I hadn't known or considered before. I also knew the other two couples better, what was behind some of their beliefs, and what was important to them. I in turn appreciated their acceptance of my views.

Higher-level empathy requires listening at that very point that listening is most difficult: when your views are being challenged or when you hear something that is actually offensive to you. It involves first and foremost an established basis of trust and mutual respect. It often requires an open identification of ground rules and certainly an understanding of the ultimate intent. Before this particular conversation started, I jokingly said something to the effect that it was nice knowing everyone. As if this would be our last conversation. Others said, "come on, we can handle this—we are just going to share views and do it nicely." That was our ground rule, and we kept to it. When you exercise assimilative empathy, you need to see yourself at par with others. Your aim should be to start out with the intent to better understand and to learn. From this more established foundation you can more successfully move to the more difficult communication challenges of resolving actual conflicts and better coexisting.

Noise

In order to exercise the higher-level communication skills necessary for such endeavors, you have to navigate through the communication distraction of what is referred to as *noise*. Noise is a pivotal construct in interpersonal communications. It refers to anything that interferes with the transmission of a message. Noise can be semantic, where meanings are confusing or misunderstood between cultural groups. For example, I moved into a new home in upstate New York many years back from out of the area. When I met a new neighbor, she told me her husband worked for the CIA. I was surprised that she offered that up so readily until I found out that the CIA stood for the Culinary Institute of America—he was a chef. He didn't work for the government in the Central Intelligence Agency as I thought. I confused meanings. Noise can also be simply physical, for example, a disruption in clarity so often experienced during a cell phone conversation prompting the ever-expressed, tiring sentence, "Can you hear me now?" Last and most potentially impeding is psychological noise. Psychological noise is interference caused by bias, prejudice, close-mindedness, and stereotypes.[11] You can imagine how, for example, psychological noise plays directly into the male-female leadership debate. There are multiple imbedded beliefs that are difficult for many to come to grips with on both sides. Think of the last conflict you encountered. What psychological noise was at play there? Everything from jealousy to too little sleep to insecurities and outright bigotry fall into this category. The chances for some form of psychological noise to enter into our communications seem endless.

If you are seeking to resolve a conflict, entrenched or otherwise, assimilative empathy becomes dicey to navigate. In addition to addressing noise elements, you are most likely going to need to compromise in some way, shape, or form. You enter into the conflict knowing that you will ultimately need to forfeit something. That puts everyone on the defensive. Defensiveness need be managed in order to get back to the business of listening, and this takes a concerted effort. Managing defensiveness is sometimes helped if you remind yourself that listening is the first step in the process and, in fact, the better you listen, the better your advantage; you know better what you are up against. If you focus instead too early on at retaining power; not losing ground, you will polarize the situation further as everyone will dig in further. At this point, you must do the opposite of what feels natural. Assimilative empathy requires faith in the counterintuitive in order to be effective. That is what makes it truly a higher-level skill set.

HIGHER-ORDER EMPATHY AS COUNTERINTUITIVE

Kathy Boockvar ran for the Eighth District congressional seat in Pennsylvania's 2012 election. I attended a "meet the candidate" session to hear Boockvar speak and learn of her views. She spoke about her background as a mediator and facilitator, helping others work toward collective solutions. She entered the race in January of 2012. She said that when she told her mother she was running for Congress, her mother was surprised, asking Boockvar how she could get into a situation that was so very broken. Boockvar's reply to her mother was "How could she not?"[12] Boockvar explained that her background and skill in mediation were precisely what was needed to unlock the grip of defensiveness and the vying for power that was the new norm in Washington. Boockvar understood, through her adept assimilative nature, the counterintuitive abilities that need to be brought to bear on situations such as these. Higher-level empathy skills tell us that we must delve in and listen attentively at precisely the moment things are most tenuous. Rather than selling our view in order to hold onto our power, we need counterintuitive attending skills in order for positive movement to occur. Listening and validating another's opposing viewpoint does not mean that we come over to their side. It does not mean that we give them more power. It does, however, decidedly lessen defensiveness and make others less reactive because they feel that they are being heard and understood. It also gives us the benefit of greater overall understanding.

Such counterintuitive, accelerated empathy allows you to maneuver through the labyrinth of noise—physical, semantic, and psychological—in order to accurately hear and comprehend the viewpoints of others. It puts you at a two-fold advantage. First, you more completely know what you are up against; the nature of the opposing side is made more transparent. Second, you can better find a window of opportunity. You can uncover where you and the other side agree and can begin to come together. Without this developed empathic acumen, erroneous assumptions can be made. The conversation can go off in a negative direction that is difficult if not impossible to recover from. If you rely solely on the might of your perspective, the divide between you and others widens. Emotions intensify, as does the actual conflict. Time spent listening does not mean that you give up your power. In the end, you can still choose to hold your ground. You can declare what is not negotiable. Better hearing of others provides greater certainty on your end as to how you can and should proceed. It also gives others an affirming sense that they are acknowledged.

Those trained to handle dire, life-threatening conflicts such as hostage negotiations employ these basic assimilative skills. Everything from labor disputes to marriage counseling benefits from the intervention of assimilative professionals. Skill as a mediator in any conflict is based on how assimilative you are: how well you recognize and address the three variables of noise, how adept your empathy and listening skills are, and how your overall judgment is based on the complete and total culling of factual data and circumstances. Mediators are expected to make recommendations to both sides on what a resolved state would look like as a result of their higher-order processing skills. The key point here is that you must work through the issues in order to resolve them, and such an effort requires turning yourself over to the other's views just when instead it feels you should hold steadfast to yours. It is counterintuitive.

A number of years ago I was learning to ski. It was a particularly uncomfortable sport for me for more reasons than we have time to address here, the least of which was a fear of heights. There I was at the top of the mountain looking down, legs locked in place, trying as hard as I could not to move a muscle. My instructor was trying to get me to lean forward and point my skis down the hill. "Is he kidding?" I thought. That was the last thing I was interested in doing. I'd go screaming down the mountain and crash for sure! I attempted to unlock my stance, leaning back instead. My legs came out from under me as I fell hard on my bottom and slid halfway down the slope. My instructor retrieved me and asked me to try again. He said firmly, "Look, skiing is very psychological, you have to manage your fears and often to do the opposite of what comes naturally." He went on to explain that if you point your skis downward and lean into the hill, you will have a more stable stance and you can control yourself better.

What he was in essence saying was two-fold. Confronting my ski demons was about reconciling my psychological noise—my fear of heights, my control issues, my views that I wasn't in good enough physical shape to do this well. It was also about doing that which was counterintuitive; by leaning into the hill, I was not losing control but gaining it. The same is true in assimilation. Leaning into the views of your opposition in order to better understand them is what you need in order to gain your stability. When the stakes are the highest, unlock that death grip on your views, stop trying to be in control and listen. Do the opposite of what comes naturally.

Imagine if more folks in Congress had Boockvar's perspective that a polarized group must shift to the assimilative, we could be on our way to more constructive resolution. Imagine the ideas that could surface, what we would learn from each other, and how we could then move to more mutual solutions. Once the assimilative foundation is set, vying for your position takes on a more civilized form. Solutions are more palpable to most as they are better balanced and better accepted. If we refer back to Foreign Minister Rabbani Khar's views as relayed at the outset of this chapter, there is hope for resolution to the complex issues between her nation and ours when both sides kindle a deeper validation of the other. This, she believes, is the basis for bilateral relationships.

WOMEN, MEN, AND ASSIMILATING

What, then, makes women adept at the assimilative? One factor is the close tie between assimilation and transformation. Transformation involves moving from one state to another. Those open to change are typically disposed to the assimilative because both involve a future state. Women have direct involvement with transformation and change in its most fundamental form. Women bear children. Throughout pregnancy, a woman's body alters dramatically. The end result is a newborn child—her child. From the moment of its birth, the woman is responsible for the care of that child. As such, mother and child come to coexist. As the child moves through its development process, there is continuous accommodation on the part of each. As infants become toddlers and toddlers move to school age, mother and child have made the necessary alterations in how they relate to each other. Before the mother knows it, her young one is learning to drive and heading off to college. Through this fundamental example, we see how women are naturally and continuously exposed to change and thus involved in assimilation in a primal way. More interestingly, women are able to witness firsthand the upsides of change. They experience their own bodies accommodating as they move through pregnancy, and they engage directly in adjustments while following their children through life—adjustments that result in enhanced circumstances for both.

This is not to say that men are not involved with or deeply moved by fatherhood. Still, though, most men have been socialized to the role of an individual responsible for that child rather than of one who leads the accommodations. It is only more recently that such social messaging in this regard is changing. Men and women are coming together to view and embrace the roles of caring for and providing for children jointly. It will take decades for this new programming to take hold. These basic differences for women— exposure firsthand to transformation along with a shared existence with their children for the good of the child's development—lead women more to the assimilative. Having more of an appreciation for what we stand to gain through change and seeing more realistically what we can and cannot control also affords women a decided assimilative edge. Overall, we are talking about a propensity for shared versus autonomous being at the root of women's assimilative inclinations. Given the interconnected world we live in today, having an assimilative edge translates to a notable leadership edge as well.

Going back to the example of gridlock in today's Congress, this clearly comes from a male-based perspective. Many of us watch and wonder what it will take—near financial ruin seems not compelling enough. If women were in charge of the group, the likelihood is that they would be more in tune to the change needed based on what is at stake. The masculine model of overcompeting instead digs in the leaders' heels and becomes more polarized. Women are more directly keyed into the concept of a win-win solution. Women who have never given birth are still socialized into a cultural group where this process is a central focus. Through images of others giving birth and their involvement with sisters and friends who do, all women participate in a powerful cultural experience. Furthermore, women see the inevitability of change, whereas men see change more as something they need to control. It is what spurs men to overcompete. Women more intuitively gauge the control factor; they come to recognize what they can and should work to control and where a greater opportunity awaits.

Men Who Are Naturals

Can men be assimilative naturals? Men who were raised in more communal ways or whose personalities or life experiences engendered them to the relational are also assimilative naturals. Men who are adept interpersonally and less dominating in nature could and would develop strong suits in assimilation. What also seems a common thread in men who are more assimilating is that they have faced some form of oppression in their own lives, much like what women routinely experience. Martin Luther King Jr. and Nelson Mandela are two high-profile examples. Men whose family and cultural backgrounds stress community over the individual would also engender more assimilative grounding. Former U.S. president Jimmy Carter, for example, had a background of humble roots and civic-mindedness. These values were instilled in him throughout his life. Noted diplomat Henry Kissinger, former U.S. secretary of state, came from a background rooted in Nazi oppression. A brilliant thinker and learner, the Harvard student and educator went on to work in government, serving as special advisor to several U.S. presidents on foreign policy matters. Kissinger served next as national security advisor and finally as secretary of state. He is perhaps a prime example of the male assimilative style in that he leveraged his intellectual ability to hone his formidable negotiating style.[13]

ASSIMILATIVE EXEMPLARS

Güler Sabanci

Güler Sabanci heads Turkey's second-largest industrial and financial conglomerate. She is also known as a key driver in evolving the cultural life of her nation. In the *Financial Times* 2010 ranking of the Top Fifty Women in World Business, Sabanci held the number-three spot, and in 2011 she moved up to number two. In the 2011 *Financial Times* write-up she is quoted as saying, "My friends call me a pacesetter. Sometimes I am impatient, I think, but you must be fast and flexible in business because uncertainty is the only certainly in life."[14] Sabanci's sentiments are those of an assimilator. There is a distinct push and pull required, a talent for knowing when to forge ahead and when to allow for accommodation. Such is the case in business and in life. She has been listed on *Forbes*'s Most Powerful Women from 2010 to 2012. She is credited with the bold and successful growth and diversification strategies for her family's business, extending beyond Turkey itself to neighboring countries.[15] Sabanci's efforts all occurred during markedly constrained financial times. Sabanci is also the recipient of numerous global recognitions, including the Clinton Global Citizen's Award, the Raymond Georis Prize for Innovative Philanthropy, the Austrian Schumpeter Prize, and the European School of Management and Technology's Responsible Leadership Award. She is also the first female member of the Turkish Industrialists' and Businessmen's Association and the European Round Table of Industrialists. She sits on the board of the International Crisis Group and the Atlantic Council and is also a member of the International Business Council of the World Economic Forum.[16] In order to accomplish what Sabanci has, a leader must possess an assimilative nature that enables one to navigate complex nuances and bring separate factions together in a way that makes sense for all concerned.

Angela Merkel

Angela Merkel, Germany's chancellor, has been at her top post since 2005. Throughout her time in power, she has been referred to as everything from iron-willed to Machiavellian to the epitome of political savvy. Most recently, Merkel is noted for the key role she is playing in sorting out the European debt crisis. Merkel seems to be the one willing to take the heat in the interest of forging a workable solution. In this sense, Merkel is working to address grossly entangled high-stakes issues. Perhaps the reason she has been described in varied ways is that she possesses diverse leadership skill sets found in those who are assimilative. She knows when to listen, when to press others, when to mediate, and when to be the clarifying voice in the room. Mostly she seems to favor accountability for all concerned, seeing to it that everyone does their part. Acting in such a manner affords her the ability to move into intertwined negotiation processes as a decisive leader.

In a recent *Wall Street Journal* article entitled "The Accidental Architect of a New Europe," Merkel is described as the crucial player in the European Union's (EU) dilemmas as she is able, in unwavering fashion, to work between the domestic demands of Germany itself and the collective pressures and needs of the greater EU. She seems well able to step into chaos and work through it in a balanced fashion, as she did in 1989 when Germany's Democratic Party was forming following the fall of the Berlin Wall. According to the *Wall Street Journal* article, Merkel is known by those closest to her for her work ethic, intelligence, prudence, modesty, hard-nosedness, ability to listen and take it all in, and open-mindedness.[17] Imbedded in this range of traits is someone who can be counted on in difficult moments to move through the confusion, involved yet somewhat above the fray, until a solution is reached. What seems noteworthy about Merkel is that she has assimilated into this high-level boys' club by displaying many masculine leadership traits while retaining key feminine strong suits as well. Perhaps the androgyny in her leadership skill is precisely what allows Merkel to do what few if any of her peers can.

Madeleine Albright

When looking at individuals for whom assimilative skill is the mainstay of their work, we think of those who serve as secretary of state. Of the past four U.S. secretaries of state, three have been women. Madeleine Albright was the first woman to serve in this role. Albright was U.S. secretary of state from January 1997 to January 2001, during the Clinton administration. Prior to that she was the U.S. representative to the United Nations, a position she had held since 1991. Albright was born in Prague, Czechoslovakia. Her family fled Czechoslovakia when it was invaded by the Nazis. The family was eventually given asylum in the United States, and Albright became a U.S. citizen while attending Wellesley College.

Albright's father was a member of the Czech diplomatic corps, and after moving to the United States, Dr. Albright was a professor of international relations. Albright's upbringing was steeped in perspectives on world affairs.[18] Madeleine Albright's tenure as secretary of state was in itself an assimilation as she worked to have U.S. foreign policy highlight women's issues globally. In a 2011 interview with Pat Mitchell on TED.com, Albright was relaxed and completely comfortable in her stature as she reflected on her time in this crucial role. Listening to her speak gave a remarkable example of the assimilative nature of women. Here are some of the highlights of what Albright conveyed:

1. Her push for attention to women's issues was not for feminist reasons but rather because, like many influential women, Albright believes that societies are better off when women are economically and politically empowered.

2. At her first UN meeting, she was with a group of 14 men. While her usual temperament would have led her to be quiet, watch, and observe as she became acclimated, she realized that if she did so, no voice would be representing the United States that day, so she was sure to speak up (contributing in that manner and acting more like her male counterparts was a great assimilative beginning for her).

3. Women are well suited to the position of secretary of state because of their relational skills along with their ability to speak directly and candidly, more so than men.

4. On matters of leadership, women change the tone and the goals of the conversation for the better in the direction of values, education, and economic prosperity.

5. The strong-suit of women is not that they bring a softer, human side to leadership but that women integrate better what has to be done with how we need to do it.

Two final potent points made by Albright need be mentioned. The first is both hopeful and rather precious when you consider the source. She relayed a story her daughter had told her recently about something her seven-year-old granddaughter said. The child quizzically asked her mother why a big deal is made about "grandma Maddy" being a woman secretary of state when from this youngster's vantage point, all secretaries of state that she knew of were in fact women.

The second point was more serious and potent. Albright told of how she formed a coalition made up of all of the female representatives to the United Nations. At the time, the total membership, men and women, was 183, and there were just 7 women. This group called themselves the "G7," and they worked as a collective to lobby on behalf of women's rights within the UN. One of their accomplishments was to influence the War Crimes Tribunal to look more specifically at atrocities against women during war. As a result, rape is now considered a weapon of war and punishable as such.[19]

Madeleine Albright leveraged well-honed assimilative skills not only to be a superior secretary of state but also to assimilate women into the fold and to push for women's issues and strong suits to be more widely and seriously considered.

General Ann Dunwoody

On November 14, 2008, history was made when General Ann Elizabeth Dunwoody became the first woman to achieve a four-star rank in the U.S. military. On August 15, 2012, General Dunwoody retired from a distinguished 38-year career serving her country. The assimilative acumen necessary for women to achieve what General Dunwoody did is clear from the sentiments expressed by the host of her retirement ceremony, chief of staff of the Army general Ray Odierno, who referred to General Dunwoody as "the epitome of the Army professional."[20] General Dunwoody is on the one hand noted for her genderless approach to her military work—seeing one cohort of soldiers rather than men and women soldiers—yet on the other hand for actively reaching out to female soldiers to assist them in their assimilation and experience as military professionals. Such a dual approach in this particular context requires an exceptionally assimilative mindset, acknowledging both that which binds and that which separates while tending successfully to both. One can only imagine the evolution of the military in the 38 years that General Dunwoody served. In an Army News Service article interviewing General Dunwoody, the general herself noted that female soldiers now lead, are awarded medals for valor, and give their lives in service. She went on to comment that their numbers are upwards of 250,000 in Iraq and Afghanistan alone, where all are armed.[21] Clearly the assimilation of women into the military was advanced significantly by the work, honor, and courage of General Dunwoody.

Güler Sabanci, Angela Merkel, Madeleine Albright, and General Dunwoody each represent different blends of assimilative leadership. Examining them together you can see a composite assimilative nature. Assimilative leaders, therefore, possess many or all of the following 10 traits:

1. Knowing how to express oneself with timing and tact; knowing when to listen and when to assert one's position
2. Having respect for those one interacts with
3. Being trustworthy
4. Being tolerant of differences
5. Being attuned to one's surroundings
6. Being open to learning
7. Able to deal with the ambiguous
8. Listening at the very point in the conversation that listening is most difficult
9. Navigating though all forms of communication noise—the physical, the semantic, and the psychological
10. Acting in a way that is counterintuitive to validate the perspective of others

Based on these 10 attributes, who would you consider to be a sound assimilative leader? Which attributes of assimilative leadership would help you become more assimilative?

BECOMING MORE ASSIMILATING

How can you become more assimilative? To begin with, you can access all of the tools presented thus far. IDEA-based leadership comes full circle here. As you progress one by one in your cultivation of the three previously identified key traits—*intuitive orientation, directive force,* and *empowering intent*—you are primed with the very skills needed to act with an *assimilative nature*. The process is analogous to a full-circuit fitness workout. You work the various muscle groups in a certain order, and as you do, your strength, agility, and resilience builds. But it isn't only the order of the workout that matters. It is the momentum that builds as you proceed. In the best of workouts, whether distance running, yoga, or a strength-training circuit at the gym, you are advised to proceed slowly in order to warm up your muscles. The workout then intensifies to a high point. Lastly, it declines in intensity, allowing your body to cool down and absorb the benefits. The same is true here, only we are working your mind rather than your muscles. Let's look over the order of the skills and tools highlighted throughout the book thus far to better call out the parallels. We will walk through the tools and techniques for becoming more intuitive, for gaining greater directive force, and lastly for becoming more empowering. We will then look to the precise manner in which you use these abilities in order to become more assimilative.

In Chapter 2 on *intuitive orientation*, the section titled "Intuition-building 101" identified the following three methods for becoming more intuitive:

1. *Quieting your mind*—momentarily stopping your forward momentum and affording a break from the constant barrage of input. Doing so opens the brain to intuitive thought and releases the backlog of mental and emotional "clutter" that can distract and undermine your overall effectiveness.
2. *Active listening*—other-focused attending in order to develop greater empathy.
3. *Reflection*—looking back over the events of the day or to a particular incident in order to better understand its meaning, what went well, and what could have gone better.

Each of these activities for intuition building serves as the mind's warm-up, positioning it best to handle the more strenuous demands to come. They are foundational to each of the 10 aspects of the assimilative nature and crucial to each.

In Chapter 3 on *feminine directive force*, the section entitled "Directive Force Toolkit" indicated the following four methods for properly exercising one's directive force:

1. *Open understanding using extension learning*—developing curiosity and an explorative mindset, an appreciation for the new and unique. The exercise called extension learning helps expand your exposure from a familiar base to something you've not yet experienced (new foods, cultures, or forms of exercise, for example). It opens one's thinking and broadens one's

tolerances, while exposure to novelty also exercises your brain, helping you draw on greater thought capacity.

2. *Planning and creativity using mind mapping*—becoming better at planning with a creative twist is crucial to complex problem solving. It enables you to move beyond linear thinking to see interconnections and answers you would not have previously considered. Tony Buzan's mind mapping is an example of an activity that affords better full-brain engagement, especially as you plan and problem solve. Mind mapping blends structured and unstructured thought in arriving at conclusions.

3. *Assertiveness-building using behavior rehearsal and chaining*—appropriate assertiveness comes from progressive practice. Behavior rehearsal and chaining provide the necessary structures to slowly build up to the optimum assertive posture. Whether your personal power is being over- or underplayed in your reactions, you can create a series of opportunities to confront matters in a way that is mutually enhancing.

4. *Accountability partners and mentors*—these are the gauges for all directive endeavors. Having someone you can count on to provide candid feedback, someone who keeps you on track, is how an accountability partner can be invaluable. Similarly, a mentor is someone who is "older and wiser." Mentors provide advice, counsel, and support. They help ensure that what you are trying to accomplish is balanced between self-benefit and the greater good.

These four skills and tools for building directive force represent the first phase of your mental workout intensification. At this point, with these skills working for you, you should feel well engaged, like a runner well into his or her workout. You are ready for further intensification and complexity.

In Chapter 3 on *empowering intent*, the section entitled "The Art of Empowering" provides what you need for more heightened demands. The three skills listed there are as follows:

1. *Shared power and influence using the six bases of power (keeping track of progress through logs and journals)*—French and Raven's work on a continuum of power is leveraged here and helps you broaden the way in which you view and exercise power. The ultimate intent is that you garner power for mutual gains. Structured logs are used to track progress as you work to amass the full continuum, while less-structured journaling helps you capture and process your thoughts along the way.

2. *Creating a culture of learning*—This is accomplished by a number of varied pursuits, including the leader openly valuing learning herself, providing structured opportunities for groups to learn together, imbedding learning practices into existing systems, and providing opportunities for storytelling where successes and failures can be discussed freely.

3. *Driving individual and team development*—this is accomplished by
    - acting from the 10 facets of grounded leadership (composed, approachable, genuine, pragmatic, cautious, consistent, stable, loyal, established, and trustworthy).
    - knowing your people and teams.
    - being involved in a development network with peer leaders and development matter experts.
    - being able to give and receive feedback effectively through practice—leveraging the techniques of behavior rehearsal and chaining just as you did with assertiveness building in order to hone your feedback abilities

PUTTING IT ALL TOGETHER

When we look to the above multifaceted series of tools, techniques, and skills, we see how they do in fact play directly into what it takes to become more assimilative. The nature of these tools is such that they each will help you become more assimilative. They are foundational and additive. In planning for your own assimilative development, take each tool, skill, and activity one at a time, beginning with those that support intuition. Engage in the intuitive tools as you would your workout warm-up until you are ready to move on and do more. Next, engage the directive force toolkit to begin to intensify your assimilative skills. Finally, move to the full complexity of empowerment to secure your assimilative abilities.

Once you feel comfortable demonstrating the three foundational skills, look through the 10 points to being more assimilative and to the situations you are trying to better impact through assimilative leadership. Create a plan for how to more directly draw from the foundational tools and techniques in order to address specific assimilative abilities. For example, if you are in the midst of a contentious situation, one where listening at the very point in the conversation that listening becomes most difficult for you, ask yourself which of the above tools and techniques could help. Could you benefit from a mentor who has been there already and can provide wisdom? Would extension learning afford you with a greater appreciation for the diversity you are encountering? This is the way to use the foundational tools to become more assimilative.

It may also be helpful to think of the various influential leaders cited throughout the book thus far, including but not limited to those who were cited for their assimilative nature. Whose stories, accomplishments, or personalities inspire you? Who would you like to emulate? Being more assimilative is akin to the cooling-down phase of your mental workout—not in that it is the least intensive but because it is crucial to your overall health and well-being. It tells you what you are capable of and what you are not yet ready for. Assimilative nature also requires more composure than it does intensity. You do have to "cool down" literally to be diplomatic and to confront at just the right moment. If you don't have command of your mental workout up until this point, you will not hold up under the demands of this final, most intricate trait. Put another way, anything you have been doing up until now that doesn't reflect the core of the IDEA-based model will come back to haunt you at this culminating juncture. Stated more positively, though, whatever you do well in terms of being intuitive, other-based directive, and empowering will come to your aid. It will drive your assimilative acumen.

CHAPTER 6

Where We Go from Here

I don't mind if I have to sit on the floor at school. All I want is education. And I am afraid of no one.

—Malala Yousufzai[1]

A NEW HEROINE IS BORN

Across the globe, a new heroine is born. Malala Yousufzai, a 15-year-old Pakistani girl, is the author of a high-profile blog against the Taliban's oppression of women. In particular, Malala speaks out in support of a young girl's rights to an education. On October 9, 2012, the young activist was shot in the head and neck at point-blank range. As Malala clung to life, a global movement began in support for her and against her attackers. Thousands peacefully protested in Pakistan, and countless groups and individuals worldwide are still rallying to her cause. Miraculously, Malala's head, brain, and neck injuries are healing. It is thought that her recovery will be long and complicated, but she will pull through without permanent cognitive damage. She continues to recover at a top medical facility in England, and as she does, a second movement is underway: this one for Malala to receive a Nobel Peace Prize, with more than 90,000 individuals to date signing the petition.

Six men have been arrested in connection with this heinous crime. One of the primary suspects who remains at large is thought to be a 23-year-old man studying for an advanced degree in chemistry. What can be said about someone who feels entitled to a graduate education and shoots a young girl in the head for wanting to take part in any schooling at all? The Pakistani

Taliban has not only taken responsibility for the shooting but vows to kill Malala if she recovers.[2] Such efforts will hopefully be arrested by virtue of the spotlight cast on this matter and on what Malala's safety represents. We begin the final chapter of *How Women Are Transforming Leadership* with an open tribute to Malala for her stunning voice and uncompromising bravery. Malala, you are an inspiration to humankind. Your life and the lives of the millions you touch are just beginning.

EMBRACING THE IDEA: FEMININE GURUS WEIGH IN

Feminist leadership perspectives support the premise of shared knowledge. In keeping with that ideal, four admired colleagues have graciously consented to convey their views on each of the four IDEA-based leadership traits. Each will tell you something about her background in leadership development and, in particular, on how she has supported the advancement of women throughout her career. Next each will weigh in on one of the IDEA-based traits. They will each then respond to a question concerning advice they would give to men, women, or organizations about the subject matter at hand. Lastly, they will share anything else they deem relevant. First you will hear from Dr. Jerri Frantzve on the trait *intuitive orientation*.

Dr. Frantzve's Leadership Background and Her Work to Advance Women as Leaders

"As I imagine many baby-boomer women share with me, I was raised with a very traditional view of leadership and women's roles. One aspect that differed for me was that *both* of my parents were salespeople who truly believed in relationship selling—that the key to selling (regardless of the product) was establishing an authentic and long-term relationship between those offering a product/service and those who needed such. Combined with the lessons learned from my former husband—an Army general who special- ized in strategic planning—I intuitively developed an integrated approach to how one moves others toward specific goals for an organization: my definition of leadership.

"My first positions within large organizations allowed me to test whatever theories I held and the application of those theories—often to disastrous effects! I remember my first leadership position within an R&D facility, where I studiously explained all the aspects of a research project to my staff. My assistant laboriously explained that she didn't care about the objectives, procedures, statistics, or potential results—she was only interested in how much money she could earn to help her grandchildren. This was my first introduction to 'situational leadership'—that one needed to develop her leadership actions contingent upon the situation(s) and the people involved.

"Throughout the past 20+ years, I have found that a balance between the relationships and the direction/strategy involved with whom we lead is the critical component of leadership. I've learned about leadership while practicing it—as a leader in the energy field, in research and development, and in academia. Of course, self-study has also played an instrumental part of my personal leadership development. I love a good theory! Once I began training leaders, as a consultant, I refined my approaches—all the while understanding that blending and balance remain the keys.

"Some of my continuous work regarding women and leadership revolves around the theme of how we use the various aspects of power as we influence others to influence the outcomes of an organization. Jung and McClelland shaped my thinking regarding power as being a force—neither good nor bad in and of itself. Rosabeth Moss Kanter's work on women and power enabled me to further develop an inclusive view toward power. Over the years the programs I've developed to help women successfully use a broad range of power strategies—depending on what is appropriate for the situation and the people—have been one of the most rewarding areas of my work."

Dr. Frantzve on the Value of a Woman's Intuitive Orientation in Leadership

"As I mentioned, I've often relied on my intuition to develop the appropriate approach to situations and people. At first, I was reluctant to label this 'intuition' as I prided myself on dealing with facts, research, and especially numbers—all far from intuitive. Or are they? A favorite saying of mine used to be 'If you can't measure it, it doesn't exist.' Once I realized that we attach numbers (sometimes arbitrarily) to constructs in order to be able to more easily evaluate them—for instance, intelligence and IQ—I became much more willing to use the label of 'intuition.'

"Much of my work has been among men. I've often been the gender 'isolate'—the only woman in the room. Initially, I struggled to be 'one of the boys'—to be seen, and treated, as an equal. I often downplayed my feminine strengths—including intuition. A male colleague noted this and offered a comment: "I'm over six feet tall. Have you ever seen me NOT use that strength or try to make myself appear smaller? You have similar strengths, so why do you choose not to use them?" It woke me up to realize that I'd been hobbling myself by not attending to my 'gut reactions.'

"So, how does intuition play a part in my leadership? I've come to understand that the 'vibes' I pick up in a situation are as important as the data I

collect—in fact, they are just another form of data. One of my research partners was reluctant to 'let' me be the data person. I felt his reluctance and
started paying attention to his body language whenever we discussed design,
data analysis, statistics, and so on. By doing so, and genuinely searching for
the source of his reluctance, I quickly realized that he had less than a rudimen-
tary understanding of the decisions we needed to make. However, he was an
expert in some other aspects of our research—where I was relatively unin-
formed. I used my intuition to risk suggesting a way in which we could collaborate that would draw on each of our strengths without confronting his
lack of statistical sophistication. Thus, he never had to acknowledge that he
was 'lacking,' he saved face, and our research partnership was a success. Was
that manipulation on my part? Perhaps. However, I prefer to describe it as
using my intuition to read the cues and coming up with a satisfactory solution
that was win-win for both of us.

"In many ways, I view leadership as a spiral rather than a linear process. In a
spiral process, I know that I'll keep going over similar ground until I "get it" and
can move on. Trusting my intuition to guide me to ask different questions, look
at a situation (or person) through a different lens, consult different experts, and
approach people in ways that are different than usual often opens the way for
unique, creative alternatives. For me, intuition and creativity go hand in hand.
When I trust my intuition that something is not as good as it could possibly
be, we often end up on a very unusual path and have a very creative solution."

What Dr. Frantzve Wants Women to Know about Leadership and What Women Need to Do Well

"We live in a time with much volatility, uncertainty, chaos, and ambiguity.
In order to lead in these times, women (and men) must be grounded in a place
of integrity; adhere to their core values about the 'right' actions and behaviors;
be nimble in evaluating situations, people, opportunities, and threats; but act
in ways that lead toward a vision for the future. To me, that means that they
must be active, not reactive; engage as many sources as possible in generating
alternatives and solutions; and 'keep the ship afloat' through these rough seas
by providing calmness, patience, humor, challenges, and rewards. None of this
is easy. Women need to go the extra mile now, as has always been the case.
However, no successful leader does so alone.

"Women need to build up a core of relationships so they have a wealth of
support and resources. The most successful leaders know what they don't
know and know how to find someone who does. Coordinating activities, asking provocative questions, trusting others to do well, and sharing success
are key approaches.

"Of course, *execution* is key. However, before one can execute there must be a vision, a plan, checkpoints, and recalibrations. Leaders need to *extend* themselves so they are as knowledgeable and diverse as possible. The old ways won't cut it, so we need to be aware of what else is going on. I recommend reading in fields other than your own; purposefully meeting people who are as different from you as possible; traveling, either physically or virtually; cultivating an active sense of *inquiry*; and trying foods, clothes, cultures, and ways of thought that are as different from your background as possible. I also think we need a sense of humor, playfulness, and fun as we lead."

What Dr. Frantzve Did That Enabled Her to Be Successful

"As I get to know individuals, I often comment that we must have had a great-grandmother in common in our backgrounds because so many of us recognize the considerable influence that a woman (or women) had in our development. I was especially fortunate to grow up living next door to my maternal grandmother. She thought I hung the moon and gave me unconditional love, support, and ice cream.

"My grandmother stopped working outside the home when she married. However, she had a profound influence on all those she touched. She approached the world with an open hand, never a fist. There was always room for someone who was hungry, in trouble, sad, outcast, and so forth. at Granny's house. She modeled a 'right way' of living and treating people by the way she lived her life, not merely through her words. It was only as I matured that I recognized all the lessons I learned from her. I owe her whatever success I have achieved."[3]

Up next is Christine Troianello on the trait *directive force*.

Troianello's Leadership Background and What She Has Done to Promote the Professional Advancement of Women

"I started my career as a clerk in a call center, answering telephones, filing, and entering orders into a computer system. A love of learning and willingness to help others learn quickly led to my first management position as a team leader in the call center and a few years later to the beginning of my career in learning and organizational development. Since that time I have specialized in helping individuals, teams, and organizations improve their effectiveness through learning, development, and other programs. I have worked in management positions from assistant manager to executive, leading teams and large global organizations. I did not want to work in roles that were classically considered women's jobs, like human resources, so I consciously avoided them. I sought out positions in other areas where women were making some inroads, like sales and marketing, customer service, product management and later in my career even supporting R&D. I have primarily worked in multinational technology companies to include, AT&T, Lucent, Avaya and Research in Motion (BlackBerry), though recently I've also worked as a senior consultant to global corporations in industries such as building products manufacturing and insurance. I am an active board member and currently president elect of the Northern New Jersey American Society for Training and Development (ASTD), an adjunct faculty member at Fairleigh Dickinson University, and a mentor to other women in their own career development.

"Over my career, I've worked for countless 'bosses' and learned a lot about what works and doesn't work in leadership, and I can pinpoint a few of them who had a strong influence on my leadership style; interestingly, they were all women. Here's some of what I learned from them:

"Seeing things quickly or differently or having a vision is not enough. You need to appeal to their minds, engage their hearts, and bring them with you.

"Build an outstanding team, teach them, and help them grow individually and as a team; trust them and don't be afraid when they no longer 'need' you. That's your chance to move on.

"Take accountability for your own development. Don't wait for a supervisor or leader to think of you for an assignment, a promotion, or a nomination for a special program, and don't be insulted if they don't. If you don't let them know what you need, you may be waiting a long time."

How Troianello Views Feminine Directive Force as a Leadership Asset

"When I've been most effective, I've found three things that work in getting things done:

"First, focus on the results, not on the actions or on 'checking the box.' As a leader, I bring people with me; I set the direction and gain their support for the vision, but after that I've learned that even if it is difficult, I need to step out of the way and let them do things their way. I never disconnect, but I work to 'clear the path' for them and help them to get results in a way that allows them to make decisions, try new things, and grow. That said, I hold myself accountable for getting results, so I hold them accountable in the same way; actions are not enough if you don't get the job done.

"Second, I believe in what I do and stand behind it. I have always had difficulty selling an idea or engaging my team unless I believed in the work or felt it was the right thing to do (ethically and morally—for the greater good). Today we talk a lot about authentic leadership, but I think I was authentic when it was not even popular to be that way. I could never completely hold back if I did not think we were doing the right thing or doing things the right way, so I take a position, even if it's not always the most popular one. This has gotten me into 'trouble' at times, but it's also allowed me to sleep at night.

"Finally, let people get to know you and don't be afraid to show how you 'feel.' As women, we're so afraid that showing emotion or, worse yet, shedding a tear is the death of our careers. What surprised me is that when it is genuine, tears of sadness, or occasional tears of anger, can be quite effective in delivering a powerful message. When my voice cracked as I delivered an honest but tough message to more than 300 people in my organization, I got more calls and messages telling me how much it meant to my team that I really cared about them. This in turn resulted in trust and support for the direction I was leading them."

Advice Troianello Has for Organizations on How to Better Represent Women at the Leadership Table

"Quotas are not working. Today, in the spirit of increasing diversity we set targets for the number of women and minorities we'd like in key strategic roles. While quotas may be necessary for some period of time or for some environments, they don't truly work if the culture is not supportive or inclusive. You may need to re-evaluate what success will look like in the twenty-first century if you want to increase the effectiveness of the business and harness the power that effective women leaders can bring to your business. Use your seasoned women leaders to help you recreate the bars by which you measure your leaders.

"Create a new way to 'play the game'; don't make your up-and-coming women compete with men to see if they can win. Men are naturally competitive and can compete about almost anything. When the rules favor their approaches and styles, they will win. I would never say that women are not competitive; we certainly are, but less on an individual level and more on a team level. This collaborative style is one that is needed to engage an up-and-coming millennial or Gen Y generation of workers, who embrace teamwork, seek support and development, and value 'giving back.' The world is getting increasingly smaller and 'flatter' and requires greater collaboration across organizational and global boundaries. Find ways to promote and value this new kind of competitiveness so that it can be a future model of leadership."

What Troianello Can Tell Us about Being Successful Overall

"My overall success can be attributed to many things, among them the following:

- Confidence: When I've been most successful, I simply believe in my own ability and don't doubt that I can figure out what to do.

- Learning: I love to learn. I learn quickly and teach others.
- Feedback: I have realized the power of feedback; sometimes if I feel myself becoming defensive, I remind myself to stay objective, open-minded, and receptive.
- Multiple interests: Both work-related and home-related. I love to run; it clears my head and helps me manage my stress.
- Coaches and mentors: My husband Jerry is a corporate business man and has been a true advocate and coach. He has taught me about business and about how men look at things; he has helped me to anticipate challenges I'll face, as well as how to leverage my strengths. I have a great family and a supportive network of friends who have celebrated with me and cheered me up when I needed it. I've also been fortunate to have had three outstanding coaches who always believed in me; it's amazing how much that has helped me. Finally, there are the teams of people I've worked with, many who have even become lifelong friends, who have contributed to my success."[4]

Next, Anita Augustine will share her views on the trait *empowering intent*.

Augustine's Leadership Background and Work She Has Done to Advance Women as Leaders

"I have enjoyed a wonderful career. I have held all levels of managerial and leadership positions up to and including senior vice president. My expertise field is in human resources, with a specialty in the training, learning, and development arenas, but I have had the opportunity to hold positions within all of the human resources disciplines. I began my business career working for the Boeing Company, and I have had the privilege of being a leader in some of the world's largest companies, including McDonald's and Wal-Mart.

"I would share the following regarding advancement:

- Do your job and be good at it.
- Understand the business and business climate of your company and organization; pay attention and listen.
- Be open, honest, and professionally direct; employees are hungry for these qualities in their leader.
- *Share*—knowledge is only power if it is shared, enabling others to benefit.
- Be academically astute, but use common sense.
- Respect your team for *their* expertise and let them do their jobs. Treat them as trusted colleagues; let them know you appreciate what they bring to the table and what they do for *you*.

"In my years as a leader, following these points has served me well. It has kept me honest and open, both as a leader and as an employee; it is easy to develop your team with these approaches, and these tips empower not only me but also my team/colleagues."

What, According to Augustine, It Means to Be Empowering and Her View of Its Value in Leadership

"For me, empowerment means trust and allowing people (including me) to do the job I was hired to do, plus the flexibility to innovate, take risks, and learn lessons. I expect this from my supervisor, and I function this way as a leader.

"Because I lead a corporate university, it is critical that our team be well versed in all areas of our business. I hold regular staff meetings and share information with great transparency. I certainly honor confidential data, but all else is shared openly. It is important that our designers and facilitators *know* what is going on; their success depends upon my willingness to be open, honest, and transparent. There is no 'guessing' regarding my opinion or position. I am clear about my stance and am honest about the company's direction as well. These approaches allow our training/learning professionals to clearly understand what is occurring in the business, what direction our company is moving, and the level of support that is being given from our university. Thus, our designers can write clearly and accurately, weaving critical business components into our curriculum, and our facilitators are masterful in addressing any contemporary issue that may arise through questions/discussions in their classrooms.

"By feeling empowered as a leader, I empower our team, through the sharing of information/knowledge. They, in turn, empower our employees, through the training and development they receive. True empowerment should create an unbroken circle of information, innovation, risk taking, and learning."

What Augustine Would Tell Male Leaders about How They Can Better Champion the Leadership Voices of Women and Why It Is Important That They Do

"I would give two points of advice for male leaders to consider:

• Actively listen
• Keenly observe body language

Too many times male leaders 'listen,' but not actively. Some women hold back thoughts and ideas or frame them within a broader context. Listen to women's responses and probe with questions for greater detail. Many women are not as assertive or confident as their male counterparts, so male leaders must be aware of this. Women's voices are sometimes softer than those of a man, and it is easy to 'not hear them.' Pay attention; too many great ideas are being overlooked because they are unheard or buried within a larger content—actively listen.

"This goes hand-in-hand with observing body language, a talent some male leaders are masterful at; others not so much. Women often look down, take notes, and do not volunteer their responses—pay attention to these body cues. *Ask* questions, call on female colleagues/team members during dialogues, meetings, and discussions; seek their opinions. This not only leads to great ideas, but it also assists in building confidence within your female business partners. Allow women's voices to be *heard*; pay attention to their body language."

Parting Thoughts Augustine Would Like to Share About What Enabled Her to Be Successful

"I have had the privilege of working for/with some great leaders. My leaders have been patient; they have been great teachers; they have allowed me to do my job, take risks, and learn from my mistakes without penalty. My greatest leaders have been open and have readily shared business information and their politically savvy tips and have helped me navigate cultural landmines. Most of all they have had confidence in me and have been an advocate for me.

"In turn, I have always performed well, through my hard work and the hard, professional work of the teams I have been honored to lead. I am a trusted colleague to my supervisors and am an active listener and coach for them as well. I am a strong team player and contributor to any team I am a member of or that I lead.

"For me, it's always been a two-way street. One has to give before they receive; one has to demonstrate what they expect to see performed; one has to walk the talk, plain and simple. All great leaders do."[5]

Our final interview is with Deborrah Himsel. You were first introduced to Himsel in Chapter 2 with her work on how to most effectively deal with feedback. On women's *assimilative nature*, Himsel has this to say.

Himsel's Leadership Background and Work She Has Done to Advance Women as Leaders

"I began my career at the Port Authority of New York and New Jersey in the late 1980s, where I led my first team. From there I worked in human resources in the corporate profit sector in varied industries, ultimately responsible for large global learning and organization development functions. I currently head up my own consulting and coaching practice and am an adjunct faculty at Thunderbird School of Global Management. My book, *Leadership Sopranos Style: How to Become a More Effective Boss*, received critical acclaim and was translated into multiple languages. I am working on my next book about the rise and fall of a prominent CEO.

"I feel fortunate to have worked in an era of postfeminism where my mother's generation paved the way for advances in women's leadership. In fact, my mother has always been a role model of leadership for me. After dropping out of high school to get married, she eventually not only got her GED but went on to get her PhD and to have both a successful academic as well as industry career. So it should be no surprise that growing up, the messages I received were that anything was possible, to always reach for the stars and follow my dreams—nothing was impossible.

"When I was in college and graduate school, I took women's studies classes, as well as classes in gender differences in the workplace. Those classes along with my experiences growing up helped to lay the foundation for my focus on developing my own career and the career of other women. I almost felt I had an obligation to continue the work begun by the previous generation.

"Early on, I did not shy away from getting involved in internal and external women's networks. Being part of a community where it was safe to talk about challenges in the workplace was helpful, especially early on. In one organization, I worked with a team of other executive women in organizing a women's leadership conference. One of the conference highlights was the organization's female CEO 'unplugged' session where she shared her lessons learned about leadership throughout her career.

"When 'Take Your Daughters to Work' was launched, I jumped in to help shape the day because of the value to young women. I also worked in informal ways to lend a friendly ear, especially for women who were working in more male-dominated environments. For example, while at Bankers Trust, I often was a sounding board for women facing the challenges of male colleagues who at times acted like they were back in their college dorm rooms, cursing and using abusive language on the trading floor.

"I held numerous roles where I spearheaded succession-planning processes. In these roles I always helped to focus the organization on the development of women for less traditional roles in manufacturing and roles with Profit and Loss responsibility. In one organization, there were many female leaders in marketing and human resources but fewer in general or country management. Consequently, we started an initiative to identify high-potential women early in their career to enable critical moves into operations and sales and roles with P&L responsibility to better prepare them for larger roles down the road.

"In my current coaching and teaching career, I have developed a special niche for taking on assignments focusing on female high-potential general managers. In addition, I have been working with women from Asian countries to find their own leadership voices while working in the more assertive, direct communication environments of U.S.-based organizations.

"Currently, I have reached out to younger women to better understand their dreams as well as challenges. My hope over the next few years is to channel some of my energy to work with young girls to help them develop leadership skills.

What, According to Himsel, It Means to Be Assimilative

"I would like to believe I was an assimilative leader throughout my early career, but sadly that isn't true. I am not sure if I was holding on to the vestiges of a command-and-control baby boomer generation or maybe just did not know any better, but it has only been over the last several years that I have truly begun to understand what being assimilative means. Learning and practicing assimilative leadership has primarily developed through my travels and working with leaders from all over the world and from some specific leadership moments from close colleagues. Over the last 12 years, I have traveled and worked in over 45 countries, continued to gain self-awareness, developed an expanded repertoire of skills, and confronted my own cultural biases. A colleague once said that the foundation of cross-cultural work was to first understand what it means to be from your country of origin, and I continue to learn what it means to be an American, especially an American who lived and worked in New York City on 9/11.

"This newfound leadership journey has also been influenced by several 'leadership moments.' Interestingly enough, several of these leadership moments have come when I have been listening to colleagues teach. For example, I had just received some of my own 360 feedback and was not rated that well on an item about being receptive to others' ideas. I thought that a bit odd as I saw myself as exactly the opposite. Then a colleague began talking about famed leadership guru Stephen Covey's characterization of advocacy versus inquiry and how the majority of our interactions are focused on advocating our own point of view and communicating what we feel is important. My colleague talked about the need to strive for a balance of advocacy and the importance of focusing more on inquiry and true listening to learn. This really struck a chord for me as I reflected on my 360 feedback and my own propensity for advocacy. Aha! I bet this was what my 360 raters were referring to. From then on, I began to approach my interactions with others in a very different way—striving for at least 70 percent of my responses being in the inquiry mode—to truly understand other perspectives. Another world had suddenly opened and materialized for me. I found that the brainstorming sessions with others were more productive and, most importantly, the outputs were of much higher quality. In cross-cultural encounters, I began to view these dialogues as opportunities to learn and ask questions about the unfamiliar. In coaching sessions, I often share this insight and technique with others with the caveat that when you are in the inquiry mode, you must be purely and genuinely curious in your questions and fully prepared to alter and shape your own point of view.

"Another critical leadership moment came when listening to another colleague teach. He said that we all needed to become 'voyeurs' of our own behavior. In interactions, we need to be participating in the interaction while simultaneously observing the dynamics of the interaction, especially the impact of our behavior on others. It's not easy to do and takes tremendous focus and discipline to be putting others' needs before your own. This phrase continues to be with me, especially in my interactions with individuals from other cultures, and has allowed me to pick up both verbal and nonverbal cues, as well as clues, and has facilitated adjustments to my own communication and behavior to ensure more effective interactions."

What Himsel Tells Others Who Have "Made It" About How They Can Better Help Other Women Advance

"Over the years I have seen such generosity in women leaders to help mentor more junior staff and also such selfishness. One of the selfish ones even said to me, 'I had to do it the hard way, by myself and so should they.' My mantra has always been to extend myself and help other women. This could mean a number of things from being a mentor, to giving advice on dress and make-up (I once went to a colleague's house and helped weed her closet of the more matronly items), to providing coaching to a younger leader on developing executive presence. When someone asks you to speak to a training class about your view of leadership, accept, even if it means rescheduling other important meetings. When you receive an invitation to be on a panel at a conference to talk about what your organization is doing to support women in the workplace, accept it. The message is to take some type of action. Doing nothing is not an option."

What Has Enabled Himsel to Be Successful

"There have been some clear patterns throughout my career. One is that I have always been the architect of my own career. I had not thought much about this until a colleague gave me a gift one day of a paperweight that was in the shape of an architect's blueprint. A bit perplexed by this gift, the colleague said that she so admired how I was always in charge and made my own destiny happen for myself. Many of my coaching clients talk about various career moves where they were 'tapped' on the shoulder for the next role. Perhaps it is my independent nature, but I never waited to be 'tapped.' No matter what the economic environment, I have always asked myself some of the following key questions:

1. Was I enjoying what I was doing? Was I energized?
2. Was I learning from my boss? If not, who else could I learn from?
3. Was I pushing and testing myself, or was I becoming stagnant?
4. Where was my 'head' at? Was it in the right place for my job?
5. Was I continuing to grow?
6. Was where I was now (with work) the best fit for where I was with the rest of my life?
7. If money were no object, what would I want to be doing?

Dependent upon my answers, I would propose other roles for myself within my current organization or leave to pursue other opportunities.

"Leaving the safety net of corporate life and venturing out on my own was in some ways an easy decision but also a scary one. I had such clarity of vision about what I wanted as a life, however, that it kept me moving forward despite ongoing worries about securing the next consulting contract."[6]

The above interviews cite powerful words from powerful women. Think about what Frantzve, Troianello, Augustine, and Himsel have to say. What are their common themes, and what distinguishing points did each make? Consider who you best relate to and what specifically will help you in your leadership growth.

With the four key constructs now solidly in mind, we move toward our overall conclusions. First, though, we get very real for a moment as we "pay" well-deserved tribute to one final woman for her success in closing a damaging loophole in the parity equation.

THE LILLY LEDBETTER ACT: SHOW US THE MONEY

On January 29, 2009, President Barack Obama signed the first new law of his administration. It was the Lilly Ledbetter Fair Pay Act. The Lilly Ledbetter Act amended the Civil Rights Act of 1964 and prevents pay-discrimination suits to be negatively impacted by the former 180-day statute of limitations period. Now, instead, with each new paycheck that reflects continued discrimination the statute date is reset. The suit is named for the woman who fought a 10-year battle against pay differences between men and women. Lilly Ledbetter initially won her case in federal court and was granted a $3 million award, but the decision was overturned in the Supreme Court because the old statute of limitations applied. Though Ledbetter lost her award, she won ultimately, for herself and for all U.S. women. She is quoted as saying, "I'll be happy if the last thing they say about me after I die is that I made a difference."[7] Clearly, Ledbetter's words are those of a woman with consummate directive force. Her empathy-based goal in her sights, she gave endlessly of herself for the greater good.

Lilly Ledbetter was born in rural Alabama. She grew up in a home without electricity or running water. As a young school girl growing up in the 1930s, she and her classmates were let out of school early to help at home with farming and the like. Ledbetter, an only child, worked every day at her grandfather's farm. She attributes this rigorous experience as foundational to her core strength and tenacity. It is written that she always knew she would do something greater with her life and so she did. Though married, she pushed the envelope early on to become a working wife and mother. In 1979, she took a managerial position at Goodyear. She was one of a few women in such roles there. Over the next approximately 20 years, Ledbetter would face discrimination, harassment, and exclusion by higher-ups and peers. She met each challenge with savvy, tenacity, and resolve. In a 2009 article by *Forbes* magazine, Ledbetter spoke candidly about what she encountered and how she responded. According to Ledbetter, in order to be treated as an equal, she developed the physical strength needed to do whatever the men did. She became respected for her efforts by many who reported to her. She learned how to work around peers and superiors who continued to resist her. She reports wanting only to do her job, be loyal to the company, and be treated fairly, but when an egregious act of inappropriateness occurred she felt she had no choice but to file a formal sexual harassment complaint.

As if this wasn't enough, as Ledbetter was close to retirement, an even greater injustice occurred. Someone left her an anonymous note with shocking information about peers who were earning 25 to 40 percent more than she was. Ledbetter reports being stunned by this harsh reality. She filed yet another formal complaint. Goodyear's response was to move the now 60-year-old Ledbetter to a more physically taxing job in an attempt to put her in her place. After 10 months she was forced to retire or risk permanent health damage. Ledbetter continued the fight, securing legal counsel. As previously mentioned, Ledbetter was awarded over $3 million in damages for insufficient wages, yet the award was eventually overturned by the Supreme Court on a statute of limitations technicality. She pressed on perhaps harder than ever, lobbying and meeting with members of Congress. She spent $30,000 of her own money, and her lawyer's fees, had he been paid, would have been 10 times as much. The end result for this activist matriarch now well into her 70s was the Lilly Ledbetter Fair Pay Act.[8] How validating it must have been for Ledbetter to stand with the president of the United States at the signing of her namesake bill and to be flanked by distinguished fellow activists such as Secretary of State Clinton and House Speaker Pelosi, who were on stage as the president spoke about the bill. Now it is up to us to see to it that Lilly's hard work is realized and continued.

WHERE IN FACT WE GO FROM HERE

Ledbetter's background and story are more than inspirational. As someone who continues to fight for civil rights, it is fitting that she be the final influential woman covered in the book. If you place her work next to that of Malala Yousufzai, you get a chilling sense for what women are still up against globally. In Malala's part of the world, the situation continues to be grave. Basic rights and safety are at stake. Women continue to be fundamentally subjugated and, worse yet, raped and brutalized in the fog and friction of civil instability and antediluvian ways. Here in the United States, a supposedly advanced nation, harassment and discrimination in the workplace continue despite law and other efforts to abate it. At best the problem is marginalized. At worst it remains rampant. The fact that the United States remains one of the few advanced nations that has yet to elect a woman into its highest offices is further evidence of the ingrained resistance at work. We came close in 2008 when Hillary Clinton ran for president. We need to continue to push until this particular milestone is realized.

Ledbetter, Clinton, and Yousufzai, along with all of the women showcased in this book, represent how women truly *are* continuing to transform leadership, but they need our help. This is no longer a women's issue; it is humanity's issue. As we work to bring women out of oppression and into the leadership forefront, the world becomes more civilized and less chaotic. More energy and cognitive capital is available to solve the world's problems and to continue to advance us all. Voices against injustices of this nature could not be loud enough. The United States and other world powers need to more fervently set the example by eradicating gender discrimination in their realms once and for all. Think of the words of Hillary Clinton when she spoke recently concerning women's rights if you need an inspiration. She said:

> Why extremists always focus on women remains a mystery to me. But they all seem to. It doesn't matter what country they're in or what religion they claim. They all want to control women. They want to control how we

dress. They want to control how we act. They even want to control the decisions we make about our own health and our own bodies. Yes, it is hard to believe but even here at home we have to stand up for women's rights and we have to reject efforts to marginalize any one of us, because America has to set an example for the entire world.[9]

What occurred in 2012 in the United States with respect to the presidential election is important to note as we move to articulate future directions. The 2012 U.S. presidential election culminated in the reelection of President Barack Obama. The Republican right was handsomely defeated. The final electoral vote tally was 332 electoral votes for President Obama and 206 for Mitt Romney. These election results served as a harsh wake-up call to the Republican Party regarding the actual world we now live in.

In an article in the *Huffington Post* entitled "Barack Obama Reelection Signals Rise of New America," Howard Fineman writes,

> President Barack Obama did not just win reelection tonight. His victory signaled the irreversible triumph of a new, 21st-century America: multiracial, multi-ethnic, global in outlook and moving beyond centuries of racial, sexual, marital and religious tradition. Obama, the mixed-race son of Hawaii by way of Kansas, Indonesia, Los Angeles, New York and Chicago, won reelection in good part because he not only embodied but spoke to that New America, as did the Democratic Party he leads. His victorious coalition spoke for and about him: a good share of the white vote (about 45 percent in Ohio, for example); 70 percent or so of the Latino vote across the country, according to experts; 96 percent of the African-American vote; and large proportions of Asian Americans and Pacific Islanders. The Republican Party, by contrast, has been reduced to a rump parliament of Caucasian traditionalism: white, married, church-going—to oversimplify only slightly.[10]

Fineman's description points to the complexity of the world *we now live in.* Simplistic ways of the past will not address such intricacy. The Republican loss further points to the constricted, overly competitive style that marks masculine-based leadership and how such a style is no longer valid; it doesn't provide the bandwidth to lead in our times. The Republicans led with their overly competitive ways in response to Obama's first-term election; they fought him tooth and nail and did so at the expense of the nation. They similarly ran their campaign with more of the same. Worse yet—so out of touch with the electorate—they chose to target the reversal of gains in women's rights as part of their platform, a positioning that not only alienated them from much of the female vote but sent a bad message to the growing numbers of minority voters about their own civil rights. Overall they lacked empathy for their constituents and by doing so paid the price in defeat. Hopefully this high-profile shellacking will help validate the broader and more inclusive fashion through which women lead and the viability of the blended masculine and feminine leadership ways needed to meet today's layered challenges.

In a November 10, 2012, op-ed piece in the *New York Times*, Maureen Dowd wrote of the disconnect that exists between the current Republican regime and the realities of our times. Regarding their underestimation of the place of women, Dowd wrote,

> In its delusional death spiral, the white male patriarchy was so hard core, so redolent of country clubs and Cadillacs, it made little effort not to alienate women. The election had the largest gender gap in the history of the Gallup poll, with Obama winning the vote of single women by 36 percentage points. . . . Romney was still running in an illusory country where husbands told wives how to vote, and the wives who worked had better get home in time to cook dinner. But in the real country, many wives were urging husbands not to vote for a Brylcreemed boss out of a '50s boardroom whose party was helping to revive a 50-year-old debate over contraception.[11]

Regarding the Republicans' disconnect with the bigger picture, Dowd noted,

> Until now, Republicans and Fox News have excelled at conjuring alternate realities. But this time, they made the mistake of believing their fake world actually existed. As Fox's Megyn Kelly said to Karl Rove on election night, when he argued against calling Ohio for Obama: "Is this just math that you do as a Republican to make yourself feel better?"[12]

Strong words, but true. It will be fascinating to see if the group will finally concede their antiquated perspectives and join the realities of the day. Only time will tell. On a more positive note, the image I have in my mind regarding the election outcome is that of former House speaker (and first female speaker of the House) Nancy Pelosi in a press conference flanked by her female colleagues announcing that she will continue as the lead Democrat in the House: a *pretty* picture.

So where in fact we go from here is to 10 very specific directives. The first five are for women and point to how they can and should continue to strengthen their leadership voice and stature. The second five directives call out what we need from all leaders, men and women alike.

WOMEN'S DIRECTIVES

1. *Strength in numbers*—There surely is strength in numbers. Women need to apply their sound networking strong suits more directly in the workplace when it comes to women's parity. Think about Madeleine Albright's work at the United Nations and the coalition of women she formed to fight against injustices toward women. It is through groups and concerted efforts such as this that greater voice and attention is given to issues.

2. *Stay the "calm-firm" course*—When you are attempting to influence others and you encounter resistance, stay the course. Remain relaxed. Don't get rattled or emotional. Be assertive; don't back down. Be even-keeled and formidable in how you approach those who are attempting to thwart you. With those who don't seem to be listening, repeat yourself in a steady, firm manner. Emotions need not be heightened; in fact, such passion at this particular juncture is undermining. It will only serve to diminish the potency of your message. There are plenty of times for passion and emotion. Think of Troianello's example of genuineness and how she leverages emotion. But when you are encountering resistance, emotion only increases the divide.

3. *Own the cause*—While in the greater scheme of things women's advancement is everyone's issue, it begins with you. This is your (our) movement. We have to set the example and keep the momentum building. It is your responsibility to create your own vision and resulting strategies for what you want to accomplish in life. This has got to be something that all women and in particular women leaders live each and every day. Here are some things specifically to guide you. Think about what you say and how you say it: What can you do to better infuse messages into your everyday speaking that positively advance the cause? What are you doing as your part of the movement? Create your own personal legacy. It can be something small so long as it speaks to giving women greater leadership presence somewhere. In fact, each of us should have multiple internalized actions that we live and lead by to help promote the advancement of women.

4. *Put a light on it*—Find ways to spotlight advances in women's rights and accomplishments as well as calling attention to injustices. Be responsible in how you call things out. Look at what has occurred around the world most recently with civil unrest being broadcast through social media and the Internet. It is harder for a negative problem to keep occurring when the masses are aware of it. Think of the support Malala Yousufzai is receiving following her attack. It is literally saving her life. What you choose to spotlight need not be on such a grand scale. You can, for example, insist that an accomplishment of a colleague be publicized in the company's internal bulletin. Every bit of attention helps. We cannot communicate enough. We must saturate conversations and communications channels with awareness of women's adept leadership ways and continue to *constructively, appropriately, and safely* call out any and all wrongdoing.

5. *Support each other*—Take a lesson from the "good ole boys" in this regard. They have raised the practice of watching out for one another to an art form. While we surely don't want to go to the inappropriate levels male leadership repeatedly has in covering up blatant wrongdoing and inadequacies (i.e., the Catholic Church and more recently Penn State's mishandling of abuse scandals), women need to more actively support each other at all levels. To share a story, years back I had just started a new job. A colleague asked to come to a dinner. She said we were going to be with a group of women from work who got together once a month. Being new, I thought it would be a great place to meet others. I was surprised when I arrived to find about 50 women there ranging from administrative assistants to executives. This group met every month at a different woman's home on a Friday evening. Everyone brought something to eat or drink.

   Overall the experience seemed social, unstructured, and fun-loving, which it was, but the more I attended, the more I could see the power inherent in the gathering. Our group was in effect the proverbial mother ship of our company. It was through this seemingly benign night out that we all learned how to really do our jobs well. The conversations revolved around the culture, issues, and real priorities of our organization. We learned who and what was doing well and what problems the organization faced. Most importantly, we learned how to get ahead and how to be recognized and successful. If you needed direction, you could always count on coming away with something that put you on more solid ground. Because of the relationships forged in this group, one needn't wait for the next month's dinner to get help either. We were always there for each other. Additionally, we were a coalition. We routinely joined forces to promote a particular view or cause. I didn't realize until much later in my career how powerful this affiliation was and how much I learned about succeeding from these amazing women.

WHAT ALL LEADERS CAN AND SHOULD DO

While women have specific things they need to tend to, there are five things all leaders, men and women alike, need to focus on. They are as follows:

1. *Assess your leadership practices*—Find ways to embrace the IDEA. Looking at the way that you now lead, find how the four key traits described throughout this book can make you a more balanced, resilient, and current leader.
2. *Use this book's tools and techniques*—Internalize IDEA leadership methods and traits into your day-to-day behaviors.
3. *Champion up-and-coming women leaders*—Get to know them and their issues as well as their strong-suits. Listen *to* them and help them become strong feminine leaders rather than trying to mold them into traditional leadership

ways. If they are really going off in a wrong direction, step up and provide constructive feedback.

4. *Don't turn your back on injustices*—Call out any and all discriminatory practices, no matter how subtle. Step up and do the right thing. Thwart discrimination and suppression in all forms.

5. *Transform the culture*—As important as it is to focus on supporting individuals, it is equally important to think long and hard about the kind of culture you want and need in order to meet your organizational goals and needs. Think about your global and virtual challenges and how to coalesce a strong team by better honing your cultural vision. Use this book's tools and techniques to get you there. It's all about embracing the IDEA.

PARTING INSPIRATIONS

It has been an honor to write this book. Researching and writing about the prominent women cited has been moving, enlightening, and stirring. In keeping with the spirit herein, I leave you with a series of quotes from some women already written about and still more who were instrumental in getting us where we are today.

> Many persons have a wrong idea of what constitutes true happiness. It is not attained through self-gratification but through fidelity to a worthy purpose.
> —Helen Keller[13]

> The reward for conformity is that everyone likes you but yourself.
> —Rita Mae Brown[14]

> The thing that is really hard, and really amazing, is giving up on being perfect and beginning the work of becoming yourself.
> —Anna Quindlen[15]

> How wonderful it is that no one need wait a single moment before starting to improve the world.
> —Anne Frank[16]

> Somewhere out in this audience may even be someone who will one day follow in my footsteps, and preside over the White House as the President's spouse. I wish him well!
> —Barbara Bush[17]

> The first problem for all of us, men and women, is not to learn, but to unlearn.
> —Gloria Steinem[18]

Never give up, for that is just the place and time that the tide will turn.
—Harriet Beecher Stowe[19]

The most difficult thing is the decision to act, the rest is merely tenacity. The fears are paper tigers. You can do anything you decide to do. You can act to change and control your life; and the procedure, the process is its own reward.
—Amelia Earhart[20]

Be bold. If you're going to make an error, make a doozey, and don't be afraid to hit the ball.
—Billie Jean King[21]

You only live once but if you do it right, once is enough.
—Mae West[22]

In keeping with the words of the immortal Mae West, go out there and do it right—feminine right—make a difference for yourself, those closest to you, and for the world. Bring your best intuition to bear. Direct things to happen and do so for the good of all concerned. Empower others—always. Lastly, take that final culminating step to the assimilative where you can help even the most divergent to come together. The result will be remarkable.

NOTES

CHAPTER 1

1. Louisa May Alcott, quoted at Feminist.com, accessed February 2, 2012, http://www.feminist.com/resources/quotes.

2. "Louisa May Alcott," Biography.com, accessed February 2, 2012, http://www.biography.com/people/louisa-may-alcott-9179520.

3. Barack Obama, "Remarks by the President at Fort Myers Town Hall," Fort Myers, Florida, February 10, 2009, accessed March 3, 2009, http://cnn.com/2009/POLITICS/02/04/obama.daschle/#cnnSTCvideo.

4. William McGuire and Leslie Wheeler, "Harriet Tubman," American History, 2000, accessed February 2, 2012, http://americanhistory.abc-clio.com/.

5. Jeet Heer, "FDR Revisited," Jeetheer.com, accessed February 2, 2012, http://www.jeetheer.com/politics/fdr.htm. "Eleanor Roosevelt Biography," accessed January 8, 2004, http://www.udhr.org/history/biographies/bioer.htm/.

6. Felder, *The 100 Most Influential Women of All Time*, 10–13.

7. "Nobel Prize Awarded—Women," NobelPrize.org, accessed February 27, 2012, http://www.nobelprize.org/nobel_prizes/list/women/html.

8. "Martha's Biography," MarthaMcSallyforCongress.com, accessed November 12, 2012, http://mcsallyforcongress.com/about-martha/martha-bio/. Ward Pincus, "Saudi Group: U.S. Service Women Must Wear Abayas," Army Times, January 24, 2002, accessed February 11, 2012, http://www.armytimes.com/legacy/new/1-292925-725903.php.

9. "Queen Boadicea," Royalty.nu, accessed February 2, 2012, http://www.royalty.nu/europe/england/boadicea.html.

10. "Wu Hou," World History: Ancient and Modern, accessed February 5, 2012, http://ancienthistory.abc-clio.com/.

11. Laura Amatuli, "Cleopatra: Femme Fatale, A Paper for Sex and Gender in Greco-Roman Antiquity," April 3, 2009, unpublished paper.

12. "Catherine the Great," World Book Online, accessed February 5, 2012, http://www.worldbookonline.com/advanced/article?id=arl00240&st=catherinethegreat.

13. Felder, *The 100 Most Influential Women of All Time*, 56–59.

14. Ibid., 126–29. "Victoria (r. 1837–1901)," Royal.gov, accessed January 10, 2004, http://www.royal.gov.uk/historyofthemonarchy/kingsandqueensoftheunited kingdom/thehanoverians/victoria.aspx.

15. "Queen Elizabeth II," Distinguished Women of Past and Present, accessed January 10, 2004, http://www.distinguishedwomen.com/bio.php?womanid=1961.

16. Neil Hamilton, "Golda Meir," World History: The Modern Era, 2001, accessed February 11, 2012, http://worldhistory.abc-clio.com/.

17. "Indira Gandhi," World History: The Modern Era, accessed February 11, 2012, http://worldhistory.abc-clio.com/.

18. "Megawati Sukarnoputri," Encyclopedia Britannica Online, accessed February 11, 2012, http://www.britannica.com/ebchecked/topic/572221/megawati -sukarnoputri. "Megawati Sukarnoputri," Wikipedia: The Free Encyclopedia, accessed March 16, 2009, http://en.wikipedia.org/wiki/Megawati_Sukarnoputri.

19. Felder, *The 100 Most Influential Women of All Time*, 194–97.

20. Ibid., 26–29.

21. Ibid., 60–62.

22. Alexander, *Fifty Black Women Who Changed America*, 43–50.

23. Felder, *The 100 Most influential Women of All Time*, 69.

24. Alexander, *Fifty Black Women Who Changed America*, 43–50.

25. Angela Hill, "Feminist Icon Steinem Laments 'War on Women,'" *Sun Sentinel*, March 8, 2012.

26. Karbo, *How Georgia Became O'Keefe*, 1–33.

27. Zengerand Folkman, "Are Women Better Leaders Than Men?" HBR Blog Network, last modified March 15, 2012, accessed March 30, 2012, http://blogs.hbr.org/cs/2012/03/a_study_in_leadership_women_do.html.

CHAPTER 2

1. Florence Shinn, quoted at Famous Quotes.com, accessed May 3, 2012, http://www.famous-quotes.com/topic,php?tid+664/.

2. Dyhan Giten, "Giten on Intuition and Healing," SelfGrowth.com, accessed September 4, 2007, http://www.selfgrowth.com/articles/GITEN2.html.

3. John L. Bradshaw and Lesley J. Rogers, "Evolution of Lateral Asymmetries, Language, Tool Use, and Intellect," *Canadian Journal of Experimental Psychology* (Ottawa) 47, no. 4 (1993): 757; Buzan, *Use Both Sides of Your Brain*, 17–18; Lesley S. J. Farmer, "Left Brain, Right Brain, Whole Brain," *School Library Media Activities Monthly* 21, no. 2 (2004): 27–28.

4. Goleman, *Emotional Intelligence*, 9-19.

5. Joseph Luft, *Group Processes: An Introduction to Group Dynamics*, 3rd ed. (Palo Alto, CA: Mayfield, 1984), 60.

6. Brandon and Seldman, *Survival of the Savvy*, 39.

7. Sharf, *Theories of Psychotherapy and Counseling*, 250.

8. Himsel, *Leadership Sopranos Style*, 89.

9. Laszlo Bock, "Women in the Google Workplace," interview by Dennis Berman, WSJ.com [audio file], May 1, 2012, accessed June 17, 2012, http://live.wsj.com/video/women-in-the-google-workplace/16A9B911-E7D9-4E1D-99E1-979CB1B0F35C.html#!16A9B911-E7D9-4E1D-99E1-979CB1B0F35C.

10. Patrick Sweeney, "Leadership: Qualities That Distinguish Women; Results from a Recent Survey Provide Evidence That Women Bring Distinct Personality and Motivational Strengths to Leadership Roles—and Do So in a Style That Is More Conducive to Today's Diverse Workplace," The Free Library, last modified July 1, 2005, accessed June 21 2012, http://www.thefreelibrary.com/Leadership: qualities that distinguish women; Results from a recent. . .-a0134301004.

11. Décosterd, *Right Brain/Left Brain Leadership*, 2.

12. Ibid., 62.

13. Ibid., 35, 62, 64, 83, 119.

14. Moustakas, *Phenomenological Research Methods*, 58–60.

15. Gillian Tett, "Power with Grace," *Financial Times*, December 10/11 (2011), 21, 23.

16. Christine Lagarde, "IMF Head Christine Lagarde Tells 60 Minutes She Has 'No Regrets, Ever,'" interview by Lara Logan, The Jane Dough [video file], November 20, 2011, accessed January 15, 2012, http://www.thejanedough.com/christine-lagarde-60-minutes/.

17. "Baby Einstein," Wikipedia: The Free Encyclopedia, accessed June 19, 2012, http://en.wikipedia.org/wiki/Baby_Einstein.

18. "Famous Women Entrepreneurs," About.com, accessed June 20, 2012, http://entrepreneurs.about.com/od/famouswomenentrepreneurs/Famous_Women_Entrepreneurs.htm.

19. Mary Bellis, "Madame C.J. Walker," About.com, accessed September 25, 2012, http://inventors.about.com/od/wstartinventors/a/MadameWalker.htm.

20. "Famous Women Entrepreneurs," About.com, accessed June 20, 2012, http://entrepreneurs.about.com/od/famouswomenentrepreneurs/Famous_Women_Entrepreneurs.htm.

21. Scott Allen, "The New Power Girls," About.com, December 15, 2008, accessed June 29, 2012, http://entrepreneurs.about.com/b/2008/12/15/the-new-power-girls.htm.

22. Indra Nooyi, "Pepsi's Indra Nooyi on Balancing Work and Family," interview by Alan Murray, WSJ.com [audio file], April 11, 2011, accessed June 20, 2012, http://www.youtube.com/watch?feature=player_embedded&v=Ft7G549GF3Y.

23. "Indra Nooyi," *The Wall Street Journal* [online], November 8, 2012, accessed October 24, 2012, http://topics.wsj.com/person/N/indra-k-nooyi/247.

CHAPTER 3

1. "Margaret Thatcher Quotes," *Dream This Day*, accessed July 20, 2012, http://www.dreamthisday.com/quotes-by-margaret-thatcher/.

2. James W. Vander Zanden, *Human Development*, 6th ed. (New York: McGraw Hill, 1997), 278; Mary Elizabeth Murray, "Moral Development and Moral Education: An Overview," Studies in Moral Development and Education, accessed July 30, 2012, http://tigger.uic.edu/~lnucci/MoralEd/overview.html.

3. Ibid.

4. Dean Praetorius, "Shin A-Lam, South Korean Fencer, Refuses to Leave Floor after Controversial Call," Huffington Post, last modified July 31, 2012, accessed August 2, 2012, http://www.huffingtonpost.com/2012/07/31/shin-a-lam-refuses -to-leave-floor_n_1724794.html.

5. Décosterd, *Right Brain/Left Brain Leadership*, 84–85.

6. Mary Lou Décosterd, *Right Brain/Left Brain President* (Santa Barbara, CA: ABC-CLIO, 2010), 91.

7. Elizabeth MacDonald and Chana R. Schoenberger, "The 100 Most Powerful Women," Forbes.com, last modified July 28, 2005, accessed August 30, 2012, http:// www.forbes.com/2005/07/27/powerful-women-world-cz_05powom_land.html; "Wu Yi," Wikipedia: The Free Encyclopedia,"Wu Yi," accessed November 20, 2007, http://en.wikipedia.org/wiki/Wu_Yi.

8. Christine Lagarde, "IMF Head Christine Lagarde Tells 60 Minutes She Has 'No Regrets, Ever,'" interview by Lara Logan, The Jane Dough [video file], posted November 20, 2011, accessed January 15, 2012, http://www.thejanedough.com/ christine-lagarde-60-minutes/.

9. Margaret Thatcher, quoted at Brainy Quote.com, "Margaret Thatcher Quotes," accessed July 20, 2012, http://www.brainyquote.com/quotes/authors/m/ margaret_thatcher.html#ZuzRzpKL2KuhKA5j.99.

10. "Biography," Margaret Thatcher Foundation, accessed August 1, 2012, http://www.margaretthatcher.org/essential/biography.asp.

11. Brandon and Seldman, *Survival of the Savvy*, 55.

12. Dan Fastenberg, "Top 10 Worst Bosses," *Time* [online], last modified October 18, 2010, accessed October 24, 2012, http://www.time.com/time/specials/ packages/article/0,28804,2025898_2025900_2026107,00.html.

13. "The United States Congress Quick Facts," This Nation.com, last modified August 28, 2011, accessed August 1, 2012, http://www.thisnation.com/congress -facts.html.

14. Sarah Palin, "Excerpts: Charlie Gibson Interviews Sarah Palin," interview by Charlie Gibson, ABC News, September 11, 2008, accessed August 2012, http:// abcnews.go.com/Politics/Vote2008/story?id=5782924&page=3#.ULPKo6V4wRl.

15. Sarah Palin, "Palin Talks Russia with Katie Couric," interview by Katie Couric, Huffington Post [video file], November 3, 2008, accessed August 1, 2012, http:// www.huffingtonpost.com/2008/09/25/palin-talks-russia-with-k_n_129318.html.

16. Buzan, *Use Both Sides of Your Brain*, 17–18.

17. "Martha Stewart," Biography.com, accessed August 2, 2012, http://www .biography.com/people/martha-stewart-9542234.

18. Deborah P. Work, "Oprah Winfrey Documentary Breaks Silence of Child Abuse," Sun Sentinel.com, September 3, 1992, accessed August 2, 2012, http://articles .sun-sentinel.com/1992-09-03/features/9201190361_1_child-abuse-child-molestation -physical-abuse.

19. Oprah Winfrey, quoted at Brainy Quote.com, accessed December 15, 2007, http://www.brainyquote.com/whosaidthat/right.html.

20. "Oprah Winfrey," Biography.com, accessed August 2, 2012, http://www.biography.com/people/oprah-winfrey-9534419.

21. "The Nobel Peace Prize 1991: Aung San Suu Kyi," Nobel Prize.org, accessed August 2, 2012, http://www.nobelprize.org/nobel_prizes/peace/laureates/1991/kyi-bio.html; John Simpson, "Burma Releases Pro-democracy Leader Aung San Suu Kyi," BBC News, November 13, 2010, accessed August 1, 2012, http://www.bbc.co.uk/news/world-asia-pacific-11749661.

22. Felder, *The 100 Most Influential Women of All Time*, 1–5.

23. Eleanor Roosevelt, quoted at Great Inspirational Quotes.com, accessed July 30, 2012, http://www.great-inspirational-quotes.com/famous-quotes.html.

24. Ibid.

25. "Hilary Clinton," Biography.com, accessed August 3, 2012, http://www.biography.com/people/hillary-clinton-9251306?page=1.

26. "Hillary Rodham Clinton: Statement before the Senate Foreign Relations Committee," U.S. Department of State, January 13, 2009, accessed August 3, 2012, http://www.state.gov/secretary/rm/2009a/01/115196.htm.

27. Heather Pearlberg, "Stocks Perform Better If Women Are on Company Boards," Bloomberg.com, July 21, 2012, accessed August 7, 2012, http://www.bloomberg.com/news/2012-07-31/women-as-directors-beat-men-only-boards-in-company-stock-return.html.

CHAPTER 4

1. Margaret Fuller, quoted at Brainy Quote.com, accessed August 27, 2012, http://www.brainyquote.com/quotes/authors/m/margaret_fuller.html.

2. "Margaret Fuller," Margaret Fuller Bicentennial, accessed August 27, 2012, http://www.margaretfuller.org/.

3. Mary Field Belenky, Blythe McVicker Clinchy, Nancy Rule Goldberger, and Jill Mattuck Tarule, *Women's Ways of Knowing: The Development of Self, Voice, and Mind*, 10th ed. (New York: Basic Books, 1997), 215.

4. Denise Cantrell, "Baby Wren," unpublished.

5. M. S. Knowles, *The Modern Practice of Adult Education (revised)* (Chicago: Association Press, 1980), 43–45.

6. "Women Matter 2: Female Leadership, a Competitive Edge for the Future," McKinsey & Company, 2008, accessed January 25, 2013. http://www.ictwomen directory.eu/digitalcity/projects/eudir/eudir_documentAll.jsp?dom=BAAFHDFD &prt=BAAEZMPO&doc=AAAATKNO&men=BAAEZMPP&fmn=BAAFJJVB

7. James W. Vander Zanden, *Human Development*, 6th ed. (New York: McGraw Hill, 1997), 169–171

8. D. W. Winnicott, *The Child, the Family, and the Outside World* (Middlesex, UK: Penguin, 1973), 17 and 44; D. Winnicott, "Transitional Objects and Transitional Phenomena," *International Journal of Psychoanalysis* 34 (1953): 89-97.

9. Patrick Sweeney, "Leadership: Qualities That Distinguish Women; Results from a Recent Survey Provide Evidence That Women Bring Distinct Personality

and Motivational Strengths to Leadership Roles—and Do So in a Style That Is More Conducive to Today's Diverse Workplace," The Free Library, July 1, 2005, accessed June 21 2012, http://www.thefreelibrary.com/Leadership: qualities that distinguish women; Results from a recent. . .-a0134301004.

10. DeVito, *Interpersonal Communications Book,* 360–363.

11. "Create a Learning Culture," Fast Company.com, July 25, 2005, accessed September 4, 2012, http://www.fastcompany.com/919023/create-learning-culture.

12. "Michelle Obama," Biography.com, accessed September 6, 2012, http://www.biography.com/people/michelle-obama-307592?page=3.

13. Michelle Obama, "Transcript: Michelle Obama's Convention Speech," NPR.org, September 4, 2012, accessed September 6, 2012, http://www.npr.org/2012/09/04/160578836/transcript-michelle-obamas-convention-speech.

CHAPTER 5

1. Margaret Mead, quoted at Brainy Quote.com, accessed September 6, 2012, http://www.brainyquote.com/quotes/authors/m/margaret_mead.html.

2. "Pakistani Foreign Minister: We're Partners with U.S.," *The Situation Room with Wolf Blitzer,* CNN, September 20, 2012.

3. Kimberly Dozier and Bradley Klapper, "Pakistan to Talk Counterterrorism with U.S., Afghans," The Huffington Post, September 20, 2012, accessed September 21, 2012, http://www.huffingtonpost.com/huff-wires/20120920/us-ap-newsmaker-pakistan-foreign-minister/.

4. "Khar, Kerry for Mutual Respect," The Nation.com, September 21, 2012, accessed September 21, 2012, http://www.nation.com.pk/pakistan-news-newspaper-daily-english-online/editors-picks/21-Sep-2012/khar-kerry-for-mutual-respect.

5. "Ann Dunham," Wikipedia: The Free Encyclopedia, accessed March 20, 2009, http://en.wikipedia.org/wiki/Ann_Dunham; Barack Obama, *The Audacity of Hope: Thoughts on Reclaiming the American Dream* (New York: Crown, 2006), 205; Mary Lou Décosterd, *Right Brain/Left Brain President* (Santa Barbara, CA: ABC-CLIO, 2010), 23–25.

6. "Obama Gets Off to a New Beginning," *Financial Times* [online], June 5, 2009, accessed July 1, 2009, http://www.ft.com/cms/s/0/3ac64d90-5136-11de-84c-00144feabdc0.html?nclick_check=1.

7. David Gergen, "Obama Speech 'Most Powerful Speech' Ever, to Muslim World," interview by Anderson Cooper, NewsBuster.org, June 5, 2009, accessed July 30, 2009, http://newsbusters.org/blogs/mike-sargent/2009/06/05/ac360-strikes-gergen-gusher-obama-speech-most-powerful-speech-ever-mus.

8. Barack Obama, "Remarks by the President on a New Beginning," speech presented at Cairo University, Cairo, Egypt, June 4, 2009, accessed June 7, 2009, http://www.whitehouse.gov/the_press_office/Remarks-by-the-President-at-Cairo-University-6-04-09/; Mary Lou Décosterd, *Right Brain/Left Brain President* (Santa Barbara, CA: ABC-CLIO, 2010), 70–72.

9. Ibid.

10. Ibid.

11. Joseph A. DeVito, *The Interpersonal Communications Book* (New York: Addison-Wesley, 1997), 16–17.

12. Kathy Boockvar, speech given at Constituent's Home, Buckingham, PA, August 26, 2012.

13. "Henry Kissinger," Biography.com, accessed September 23, 2012, http://www.biography.com/people/henry-kissinger-9366016?page=3.

14. Andrew Hill, "The Top 50 Women in World Business 2011," *Financial Times* (insert), November 15 (2011), 8.

15. "Guler Sabanci," Forbes.com, accessed October 8, 2012, http://www.forbes.com/profile/guler-sabanci/.

16. "President Clinton to Honor Recipients of the Fifth Annual Clinton Global Citizen Award," Clinton Global Initiative [press release], September 22, 2011, accessed October 14, 2012, http://press.clintonglobalinitiative.org/press_releases/president-clinton-to-honor-recipients-of-the-fifth-annual-clinton-global-citizen-awards/.

17. Matthew Kaminski, "The Accidental Architect of a New Europe," *Wall Street Journal*, September 26, 2012, A19.

18. "Madeleine K. Albright," *The New York Times* [online], January 11, 2013, accessed October 8, 2012, http://topics.nytimes.com/topics/reference/timestopics/people/a/madeleine_k_albright/index.html.

19. Madeleine Albright, "Madeleine Albright: On Being a Woman and a Diplomat," interview by Pat Mitchell, Ted.com, December 20, 2010, accessed October 8, 2012, http://www.ted.com/talks/madeleine_albright_on_being_a_woman_and_a_diplomat.html.

20. C. Todd Lopez, "First Female Four-Star General Retires from Army," www.Army.Mil, August 15, 2012, accessed October 14, 2012, http://www.army.mil/article/85606/.

21. Ibid.

CHAPTER 6

1. Nasir Habib and Saima Mohsin, "Arrests Made in Shooting of Pakistani Schoolgirl Malala," CNN World, October 28, 2012, accessed October 29, 2012, http://www.cnn.com/2012/10/24/world/pakistan-malala-shooting/index.html.

2. Ibid.

3. Jerri Frantzve, interview by the author, October 20, 2012.

4. Christine Troianello, interview by author, November 9, 2012.

5. Anita Augustine, interview by author, November 2, 2012.

6. Deborrah Himsel, interview by author, November 4, 2012.

7. "The Lilly Ledbetter Fair Pay Act," Lilly Ledbetter.com, accessed November 4, 2012, http://www.lillyledbetter.com.

8. Heidi Brown, "Equal Pay for Lilly Ledbetter," Forbes.com, April 28, 2009, accessed November 5, 2012, http://www.forbes.com/2009/04/28/equal-pay-discrimination-forbes-woman-leadership-wages.html.

9. Jesse Ellison, "Women in the World Summit: Most Memorable Quotes," The Daily Beast, March 16, 2012, accessed November 8, 2012, http://www .thedailybeast.com/articles/2012/03/16/women-in-the-world-summit-most-memorable-quotes.html.

10. Howard Fineman, "Barack Obama Reelection Signals Rise of New America," The Huffington Post, November 6, 2012, accessed November 8, 2012, http://www .huffingtonpost.com/2012/11/06/barack-obama-reelection_n_2085819.html.

11. Maureen Dowd, "Romney Is President," *The New York Times* [online], November 10, 2012, accessed November 12, 2012, http://www.nytimes.com/2012/ 11/11/opinion/sunday/dowd-romney-is-president.html?_r=0.

12. Ibid.

13. "10 Awesome Quotes from Influential Women," Coming Out Christian [blog], March 8, 2012, accessed November 2012, http://cmgoutchristian. wordpress.com/2012/03/02/10-awesome-quotes-from-influential-women/.

14. Ibid.

15. Ibid.

16. Ibid.

17. "Women's History Inspirations," Biography.com, accessed November 8, 2012, http://www.biography.com/tv/classroom/womens-history-inspirations.

18. "Inspiring Quotes by Women," Feminist.com, accessed November 8, 2012, http://www.feminist.com/resources/quotes/.

19. Simran Khurana, "Motivational Quotes by Women," About.com, accessed November 8, 2012, http://quotations.about.com/od/morepeople/a/woman4.htm.

20. Reena Davis, "Inspirational Quotes by Famous Women to Celebrate National Women's History Month," Yahoo! Voices, February 17, 2011, accessed November 8, 2012, http://voices.yahoo.com/inspirational-quotes-famous-women-celebrate-7881 616.html?cat=74.

21. Tara Holling, "Top 50 Inspirational Quotes for Women Entrepreneurs (by Women!)," Entreprenista, July 22, 2011, accessed November 8, 2012, http:// entreprenista.com/2011/07/top-50-inspirational-quotes-for-women-entrepreneurs -by-women/.

22. Ibid.

BIBLIOGRAPHY

Alexander, Amy. *Fifty Black Women Who Changed America*. New York: Kensington, 1999.

Allen, Scott. "The New Power Girls." About.com. December 15, 2008. Accessed June 29, 2012. http://entrepreneurs.about.com/b/2008/12/15/the-new-power-girls.htm.

Belenky, Mary Field, Blythe McVicker Clinchy, Nancy Rule Goldberger, and Jill Mattuck Tarule. *Women's Ways of Knowing. The Development of Self, Voice, and Mind*. 10th ed. New York: Basic Books, 1997.

Bock, Laszlo. "Women in the Google Workplace." Interview by Dennis Berman. WSJ.com [audio file]. May 1, 2012. Accessed June 17, 2012. http://live.wsj.com/video/women-in-the-google-workplace/16A9B911-E7D9-4E1D-99E1-979CB1B0F35C.html#!16A9B911-E7D9-4E1D-99E1-979CB1B0F35C.

Bradshaw, John L., and Lesley J. Rogers. "The Evolution of Lateral Asymmetrics, Language, Tool Use, and Intellect." *Canadian Journal of Experimental Psychology* 47, no. 4 (1993): 757.

Brandon, Rick, and Marty Seldman. *Survival of the Savvy: High-Integrity Political Tactics for Career and Company Success*. New York: Free Press, 2004.

Brown, Heidi. "Equal Pay for Lilly Ledbetter." Forbes.com. April 28, 2009. Accessed November 5, 2012. http://www.forbes.com/2009/04/28/equal-pay-discrimination-forbes-woman-leadership-wages.html.

Buzan, Tony. *Use Both Sides of Your Brain: New Mind-Mapping Techniques*. 3rd ed. New York: Plume, 1991.

"Create a Learning Culture." Fast Company.com. July 25, 2005. Accessed September 4, 2012. http://www.fastcompany.com/919023/create-learning-culture.

Décosterd, Mary Lou. *Right Brain/Left Brain Leadership: Shifting Style for Maximum Impact*. Westport, CT: Praeger, 2008.

Décosterd, Mary Lou. *Right Brain/Left Brain President: Barack Obama's Uncommon Leadership Ability and How We Can Each Develop It*, Santa Barbara, CA, 2010.

DeVito, Joseph A. *The Interpersonal Communications Book*. 8th ed. New York: Longman, 1998.

Dowd, Maureen. "Romney Is President." NYTimes.com. Last modified November 10, 2012. Accessed November 12, 2012. http://www.nytimes.com/2012/11/11/opinion/sunday/dowd-romney-is-president.html?_r=0.

Dozier, Kimberly, and Bradley Klapper. "Pakistan to Talk Counterterrorism with US, Afghans." Huffington Post. Last modified September 20, 2012. Accessed September 21, 2012. http://www.huffingtonpost.com/huff-wires/20120920/us-ap-newsmaker-pakistan-foreign-minister/.

Ellison, Jesse. "Women in the World Summit: Most Memorable Quotes." The Daily Beast. March 16, 2012. Accessed November 8, 2012. http://www.thedailybeast.com/articles/2012/03/16/women-in-the-world-summit-most-memorable-quotes.html.

Farmer, Lesley S. J. "Left Brain, Right Brain, Whole Brain." *School Library Media Activities Monthly* 21, no. 2 (2004): 27–28.

Fastenberg, Dan. "Top 10 Worst Bosses." Time.com. October 18, 2012. Accessed October 24, 2012. http://www.time.com/time/specials/packages/article/0,28804,2025898_2025900_2026107,00.html.

Felder, Deborah G. *The 100 Most Influential Women of All Time*. Updated and revised. New York: Citadel Press, 2001.

Fineman, Howard. "Barack Obama Reelection Signals Rise of New America." Huffington Post. November 6, 2012. Accessed November 8, 2012. http://www.huffingtonpost.com/2012/11/06/barack-obama-reelection_n_2085819.html.

Gergen, David. "Obama Speech 'Most Powerful Speech' Ever, to Muslim World." Interview by Anderson Cooper. NewsBuster.org. June 5, 2009. Accessed July 30, 2009. http://newsbusters.org/blogs/mike-sargent/2009/06/05/ac360-strikes-gergen-gusher-obama-speech-most-powerful-speech-ever-mus.

Goleman, Daniel. *Emotional Intelligence: Why It Can Matter More Than IQ*. New York: Bantam Books, 1995.

Habib, Nasir, and Salma Mohsin. "Arrests Made in Shooting of Pakistani Schoolgirl Malala." CNN.com. October 28, 2012. Accessed October 29, 2012. http://www.cnn.com/2012/10/24/world/pakistan-malala-shooting/index.html.

Heer, Jeet. "FDR Revisited." Jeetheer.com. February 2004. Accessed February 2, 2012. http://www.jeetheer.com/politics/fdr.htm.

Hill, Andrew. "The Top 50 Women in World Business 2011." *Financial Times*, November 15, 2011, 8.

Hill, Angela. "Feminist Icon Steinem Laments 'War on Women.'" *Sun Sentinal*, March 8, 2012, 7A.

Himsel, Deborrah. *Leadership Sopranos Style: How to Become a More Effective Boss*. Chicago: Dearborn, 2003.

Kaminski, Matthew. "The Accidental Architect of a New Europe." *The Wall Street Journal*, September 26, 2012, A19.

Karbo, Karen. *How Georgia Became O'Keefe: Lessons on the Art of Living*. Guilford, CT: Globe Pequot, 2012.

"Khar, Kerry for Mutual Respect." The Nation.com. September 21, 2012. Accessed September 21, 2012. http://www.nation.com.pk/pakistan-news-newspaper-daily-english-online/editors-picks/21-Sep-2012/khar-kerry-for-mutual-respect.

Knowles, M. S. *The Modern Practice of Adult Education (revised)*. N.p.: Chicago: Association Press, 1980.

Lagarde, Christine. "IMF Head Christine Lagarde Tells 60 Minutes She Has 'No Regrets, Ever.'" Interview by Lara Logan. The Jane Dough [video file]. November 20, 2011. Accessed January 15, 2012. http://www.thejanedough.com/christine-lagarde-60-minutes/.

Levy, Jerre. "Possible Basis for the Evolution of Lateral Specialization of the Human Brain." *Nature* 224, no. 5219 (1969): 614–615.

Lopez, C. Todd. "First Female Four-Star General Retires from Army." United States Army. August 15, 2012. Accessed October 14, 2012. http://www.army.mil/article/85606/.

Luft, Joseph. *Group Processes: An Introduction to Group Dynamics*. 3rd ed. Palo Alto, CA: Mayfield, 1984.

MacDonald, Elizabeth, and Chana R. Schoenberger. "The 100 Most Powerful Women." Forbes.com. July 28, 2005. Accessed August 30, 2012. http://www.forbes.com/2005/07/27/powerful-women-world-cz_05powom_land.html.

"Madeleine Albright: On Being a Woman and a Diplomat." Ted.com [video file]. December 20, 2010. Accessed October 8, 2012. http://www.ted.com/talks/madeleine_albright_on_being_a_woman_and_a_diplomat.html.

Moustakas, Clark. *Phenomenological Research Methods*. Thousand Oaks, CA: Sage, 1994.

Murray, Mary Elizabeth. "Moral Development and Moral Education: An Overview." Studies in Moral Development and Education. Accessed July 30, 2012. http://tigger.uic.edu/~lnucci/MoralEd/overview.html.

"Nomination Hearing to Be Secretary of State: Statement of Hillary Rodham Clinton." Accessed August 3, 2012. http://www.state.gov/secretary/rm/2009a/01/115196.htm.

Nooyi, Indra. "Pepsi's Indra Nooyi on Balancing Work and Family." Interview by Alan Murray. WSJ.com [audio file]. April 11, 2011. Accessed June 20, 2012. http://www.youtube.com/watch?v=Ft7G549GF3Y.

Nowak, Rachel. "Nerve Cells Mirror Brain's Left-Right Divide." *New Scientist* 178, no. 2395 (2003): 20.

Obama, Barack. *The Audacity of Hope: Thoughts on Reclaiming the American Dream*. New York: Crown, 2006.Obama, Barack. "Remarks by the President at Fort Myers Town Hall." CNN Politics.com. Accessed March 3, 2009. http://cnn.com/2009/POLITICS/02/04/obama.daschle/#cnnSTCvideo.

Obama, Barack. "Remarks by the President on a New Beginning." Speech presented at Cairo University, Cairo, Egypt, June 4, 2009. Accessed June 7, 2009. http://www.whitehouse.gov/the_press_office/Remarks-by-the-President-at-Cairo-University-6-04-09/.

"Obama Gets Off to a New Beginning." *Financial Times* [online]. June 5, 2009. Accessed July 1, 2009. http://www.ft.com/cms/s/0/3ac64d90-5136-11de-84c-00144feabdc0.html?nclick_check=1.

Obama, Michelle. "Transcript: Michelle Obama's Convention Speech." NPR. September 4, 2012. Accessed September 6, 2012. http://www.npr.org/2012/09/04/160578836/transcript-michelle-obamas-convention-speech.

Palin, Sarah. "Excerpts: Charlie Gibson Interviews Sarah Palin." Interview by Charlie Gibson. ABC News. September 11, 2008. Accessed August 2012. http://abcnews.go.com/Politics/Vote2008/story?id=5782924&page=3#.ULPKo6V4wRl.

Palin, Sarah. "Palin Talks Russia with Katie Couric." Interview by Katie Couric. Huffington Post [video file]. November 3, 2008. Accessed August 1, 2012. http://www.huffingtonpost.com/2008/09/25/palin-talks-russia-with-k_n_129318.html.

""Perlberg, Heather. "Stocks Perform Better If Women Are on Company Boards." Bloomberg.com. July 21, 2012. Accessed August 7, 2012. http://www.bloomberg.com/news/2012-07-31/women-as-directors-beat-men-only-boards-in-company-stock-return.html.

Pincus, Ward. "Saudi Group: U.S. Servicewomen Must Wear Abayas." Army Times. January 24, 2002. Accessed February 11, 2012. http://www.armytimes.com/legacy/new/1-292925-725903.php.

Praetorius, Dean. "Shin A-Lam, South Korean Fencer, Refuses to Leave Floor after Controversial Call." Huffington Post. July 31, 2012. Accessed August 2, 2012. http://www.huffingtonpost.com/2012/07/31/shin-a-lam-refuses-to-leave-floor_n_1724794.html.

"President Clinton to Honor Recipients of the Fifth Annual Clinton Global Citizen Award." Clinton Global Initiative [press release]. September 22, 2011. Accessed October 14, 2012. http://press.clintonglobalinitiative.org/press_releases/president-clinton-to-honor-recipients-of-the-fifth-annual-clinton-global-citizen-awards/.

Rennie, John, ed. "The Hidden Mind." Special issue. *Scientific American*, December 2002, 26–31.

Sharf, Richard S. *Theories of Psychotherapy and Counseling: Concepts and Cases.* Pacific Grove, CA: Brooks/Cole, 1996.

Simpson, John. "Burma Releases Pro-democracy Leader Aung San Suu Kyi." BBC News. November 13, 2010. Accessed August 1, 2012. http://www.bbc.co.uk/news/world-asia-pacific-11749661.

Springer, Sally P., and Georg Deutsch. *Left Brain, Right Brain: Perspectives from Cognitive Neuroscience.* 5th ed. New York: W.H. Freeman, 1998.

Sousa, David A. *How the Brain Learns.* 2nd ed. Thousand Oaks, CA: Corwin Press, 2000.

Tett, Gillian. "Power with Grace." *Financial Times*, December 10/11, 2011, 21, 23.

Vander Zanden, James W. *Human Development.* 6th ed. New York: McGraw Hill, 1997.

"Victoria (r. 1837–1901)." Royal.gov. Accessed January 10, 2004. http://www.royal.gov.uk/historyofthemonarchy/kingsandqueensoftheunitedkingdom/thehanoverians/victoria.aspx.

Winnicott, D. W. *The Child, the Family, and the Outside World.* Reading, MA: Addison-Wesley, 1987.

"Women Matter 2: Female Leadership, a Competitive Edge for the Future." McKinsey & Company. 2008. Accessed August 28, 2012. http://www.ictwomendirectory.eu/digitalcity/projects/eudir/eudir_documentAll.jsp?dom=BAAFHDFD&prt=BAAEZMPO&doc=AAAATKNO&men=BAAEZMPP&fmn=BAAFJJVB.

Work, Deborah. "Oprah Winfrey Documentary Breaks Silence of Child Abuse."
    Sun Sentinel.com. September 3, 1992. Accessed August 2, 2012. http://articles
    .sun-sentinel.com/1992-09-03/features/9201190361_1_child-abuse-child-molestation
    -physical-abuse.
Zenger, Jack, and Joseph Folkman. "Are Women Better Leaders than Men?" HBR
    Blog Network. March 15, 2012. Accessed March 30, 2012. http://blogs.hbr.org/
    cs/2012/03/a_study_in_leadership_women_do.html.

INDEX

Accountability partner, as development tool, 65, 114

Active listening, as development tool, 38–40, 76–77, 87, 102

Adult learning, 81. *See also* Knowles, Malcolm

Aigner-Clarke, Julie, 42. *See also* Entrepreneurship; Intuitive orientation: exemplars

Albright, Madeleine, 110–12, 135. *See also* Assimilative nature: exemplars

Alcott, Louisa May, 1

Alter-brain behavior, 38

Andragony, 81. *See also* Knowles, Malcolm

Androgyny, 3, 81. *See also* Gender-integrated leadership

Anthony, Susan B., 20–21

Ash, Mary Kay, 42. *See also* Entrepreneurship and the new power girls; Intuitive orientation: exemplars

Assertiveness: assertive counterbalance, 56–58; assertive impact, 65; assertive leader, 62; assertiveness building, 64–65, 114; assertiveness to excess, 58–60; overly assertive pitfall—treating assumptions as facts, 60–62; traits of assertive leadership, 54–55

Assimilative nature: becoming more assimilative, 112–16; as empathy to the max, 102–3; exemplars, 108–12; in higher-level communication, 103–6; Himsel interview on, 126–30; how men and women differ, 107–8; key feminine leadership trait, 25, 95–99; mother-to-child heritage, 99–102. *See also* Dunham, Ann; Obama, Barack, mother-to-son heritage; Himsel, Deborrah

Augustine, Anita, interview on empowering intent, 124–26

Awareness: as development tool; blind awareness/blind spots, 31–35; as feminine leadership quality, 36–37; hidden awareness, 31–33; open awareness, 31, 33; self- and other-awareness, 27, 30–31, 34

Baker, Ella, 21–23

Behavior rehearsal, as development tool, 64, 114. *See also* Assertiveness

Belenky, Mary Field, Feminist perspective on
learning of, 75. *See also* Shared knowledge;
Shared mastery; Shared power
Berman, Dennis, Women in the Economy
Conference interview with Lazzlo Bock,
36. *See also* Bock, Lazzlo
Bethune, Mary McLeod, 21–22
Blind awareness, 31, 33; blind spots,
32, 34, 35
Bock, Lazzlo, Interview on women,
promotions, and awareness, 36–37
Boockvar, Kathy, 104–6
Boudicca, 12–14, 16
Bowlby, John, 83–84. *See also* Maternal
attachment
Brandon, Rick, on political savvy, 32, 58
Brown, Rita Mae, 137
Bush, Barbara, 137
Buzan, Tony, 63–64. *See also* Mind
mapping, as development tool

Carter, Jimmy, 108. *See also* Assimilative
nature: exemplars
Catherine the Great, 17
Catt, Carrie Chapman, 21
Chaining, as development tool, 64, 114. *See
also* Assertiveness building
Challenger disaster, 31, 33
Chao, Wu, 13–14, 16
Cleopatra, 13, 16–17
Clinchy, Blythe McVicker, feminist
perspective on learning, 75. *See also*
Shared knowledge; Shared mastery;
Shared power
Clinton, Hilary Rodham, 17, 69–70,
132–33. *See also* Directive force:
exemplars
Collective orientation, 48, 78–80, 86;
versus siloes, 79
Competing, healthy masculine leadership
trait versus detriment, 7–8
Contrition, healthy feminine leadership
trait versus detriment, 4–7
Cooper, Anderson, interview with Barack
Obama, 5–6. *See also* Obama, Barack:
healthy contrition in a leader
Couric, Katie, interview with Sarah Palin,
61. *See also* Palin, Sarah

Creativity building, 63, 113. *See also*
Directive force: tool kit
Credit Suisse Research Institute, 71
Culture of learning, 89–90, 92, 114

Development tools. *See* accountability
partners; Active listening; Awareness;
Behavior rehearsal; Chaining;
Creativity-building; Drawing; Empathy;
Extension learning; Journal; Log;
Mentors; Mind mapping; Planning;
Quieting the mind; Reflection
Directive force: and assertiveness, 54–62;
defining features of, 47–50; and
empathy-guided drive, 77; exemplars,
65–70; five key elements of, 53–54;
informed by intuition, 95; as key feminine leadership trait, 25, 45, 51–52;
masculine versus feminine brand, 70–71;
moral underpinnings of, 50–53; tie-in to
assimilative nature, 112–13; tool kit,
62–65; Troianello interview on, 21–24.
See also Assertiveness; Intuition; Moral
development; Troianello, Christine
Double standard/double blind, 13–14; how
to mitigate, 15
Dowd, Maureen, on underestimating the
place of women, 134
Drawing, as development tool, 64. *See also*
Creativity building
Dunham, Ann, 99–102
Dunwoody, General Ann, 111–12. *See also*
Assimilative nature: exemplars

Earhart, Amelia, 138
Emotional intelligence, 30, 76. *See also*
Goleman, Daniel
Empathy: as development tool, 33, 63;
empathic acumen, 40; empathic purpose,
53; empathy-guided drive, 77; higher-
level empathy, 102–6
Empowering intent: the art of, 87–92; and
assimilative nature, 112; Augustine,
Anita, interview on, 124–36; and
collective power, 86–87; exemplars,
92–95; how to empower, 74–79; as key
feminine leadership trait, 21, 71, 73, 95;
and maternal attachment, 82–85; and

shared knowledge, 74–76, 90 ; and
shared mastery, 74–76; and shared
power, 87–90, 114, 124; and
sustainability, 80–82. *See also*
Assimilative nature; Augustine, Anita:
interview on empowering intent;
Maternal attachment; Shared
knowledge; Shared mastery; Shared
power
Entrepreneurship and the new power girls,
42–45. *See also* Aigner-Clark, Julie; Ash,
Mary Kay; Fields, Debbie; Roddick,
Anita; Stewart, Martha; Walker,
Madame C. J.; Winfrey, Oprah
Experiential learning, 75
Extension learning, as development tool,
63, 113–14. *See also* Directive force:
tool kit

Feedback, 32–36, 77, 91, 115. *See also*
Himsel, Deborrah
Feminine leadership traits, 3. *See also*
Assimilative nature; Directive force;
Empowering intent; Intuitive
orientation
Fields, Debbie, 42. *See also*
Entrepreneurship and the new
power girls; Intuitive orientation:
exemplars
Fineman, Howard, on rise of new
America, 133–34. *See also*
Obama, Barack: reelection
indicative of new America
Folkman, Joseph, and leadership
effectiveness, 24–25
Frank, Anne, 137
Frantzve, Jerri, 118–21
French, John, 87
Fuller, Margaret, 73, 81

Gandhi, Indira, 18–19
Gender-integrated leadership, 3. *See also*
Androgyny
Gergen, David, on Obama's speech to the
Muslim world, 100. *See also* Obama,
Barack: mother-to-son heritage
Gestalt psychology, 32–33. *See also*
Awareness

Gibson, Charles, interview with Sarah
Palin. *See also* Palin, Sarah
Gilligan, Carol, 51, 53
Giten, Dyhan, 27, 30
Goldberger, Nancy Rule, and feminist
perspective on learning, 75. *See also*
Shared knowledge; Shared mastery;
Shared power
Goleman, Daniel, 30. *See also* Emotional
intelligence
Good enough mother, 84. *See also*
Winnicott, Donald
"Good ole boys" club, 3, 136. *See also*
Over competing, as masculine leadership
detriment; Resistance, as culturally
embedded
Greenberg, Herbert, and leadership
qualities that distinguish women, 37, 85
Grounded leader, 91

Hay, Mary Garret, 21
Heterogeneous group, 86
Hidden agendas, 32
Hidden awareness, 31–33
Himsel, Deborrah, 36, 126–30. *See also*
Feedback
Holding environment, 83–84. *See also*
Winnicott, Donald
Homogeneous group, 86

IDEA-based leadership, 25–26, 62, 95; and
assimilative nature, 112, 118; and directive force, 63; and empowering intent,
71; and gender-integrated leadership,
136–37; and intuitive orientation, 76,
118–21;. *See also* Assimilative nature;
Directive force; Empowering intent;
Feminine leadership traits; Intuitive
orientation
Individual development, as a function of
leadership, 82, 90–92, 115
Ingham, Harry, 31. *See also* Awareness:
self- and other- awareness
Intuition, 27–29, 37, 40–41, 44; intuition
building, 38–40, 113; women's intuition,
27–28, 36, 45. *See also* Active listening,
as development tool; Intuitive
orientation; Quieting the mind, as

development tool; Reflection, as
  development tool
Intuitive, 28, 32–33, 37–38, 40–42,
  44–45, 63
Intuitive orientation: and awareness,
  31–38; exemplars, 40–44; Frantzve
  interview on, 118–21; how to develop,
  40; as key feminine leadership trait, 20,
  27–29; as related to leadership today,
  29–31; tie-in to assimilative nature, 95,
  112; tie-in to directive force, 44–45;
  tie-in to empowering intent, 76. See also
  Awareness; Emotional intelligence;
  Frantzve, Jerri; Intuition; Intuitive

Journal, as development tool, 88, 114

Keller, Helen, 137
Khar, Rabbini, 97–98, 106
King, Billy Jean, 23, 138
King, Martin Luther, Jr., 22, 108. See also
  Assimilative nature: exemplars
Kissinger, Henry, 108. See also Assimilative
  nature: exemplars
Knowles, Malcolm, 81–82
Kohlberg, Lawrence, 50–51, 53
Kyi, Aung San Suu, 67–68. See also
  Directive force: exemplars

Lagarde, Christine, 40–42, 44–45. See also
  Intuitive orientation: exemplars
Lam, Shin A., 52–53
Leadership: cultural origins and
  underpinnings, 2–3; male versus female
  success traits in, 24–25, 135; masculine
  versus feminine preferences in, 2–9;
  practices, 136. See also Assertiveness:
  traits of assertive leadership; Competing:
  as healthy masculine leadership trait
  versus detriment; Contrition: as healthy
  feminine leadership trait versus
  detriment; Feminine leadership traits;
  Folkman, Joseph, and leadership
  effectiveness; Greenberg, Herbert, and
  leadership qualities that distinguish
  women; Grounded leader; IDEA-based
  leadership; Obama, Barack:
  androgynous leadership; Sweeney,

Patrick, and leadership qualities that
  distinguish women; Zenger, Jack, and
  leadership effectiveness
Learning lens, and how women approach
  leadership, 4–7
Ledbetter, Lilly, 130–32
Left brain: directive force and, 45, 49, 62; as
  synergistic, 64; traits, 28–29, 38, 40. See
  also Alter-brain behavior
Lilly Ledbetter Fair Pay Act, 130–32
Log, as development tool, 88, 114
Logan, Lara, interview with Christine
  Lagarde, 41. See also Lagarde,
  Christine
Luft, Joseph, 31. See also Awareness:
  self- and other- awareness

Mahr, Bill, 62. See also Assertiveness:
  overly assertive pitfall—treating
  assumptions as facts
Mandela, Nelson, 108. See also Assimilative
  nature: exemplars
Maternal attachment, 83–85
McLeod, Mary, 21–22
McKinsey and Company, and gender
  diversity as a corporate driver, 82–83, 85
McSally, Martha, 11–12, 14
Mead, Margaret, 97, 99
Megawati, 18–20
Meir, Golda, 18–19
Mentors, as development tool, 65, 114
Merkel, Angela, 109–10, 112. See also
  Assimilative nature: exemplars
Mind mapping, as development tool, 63–64,
  113. See also Buzan, Tony
Mitchell, Pat, interview with Madeleine
  Albright, 110. See also Albright,
  Madeleine
Moral development: male versus female
  orientations, 50–53; social justice versus
  social care, 50–53; stages of, 50–51. See
  also Gilligan, Carol; Kohlberg, Lawrence
Mother Theresa, 23–24

9/11, 31, 33
Nobel prize: Aung San Suu Ky as Peace
  Prize recipient, 67; Mother Theresa as
  Peace Prize recipient, 23; women

laureates, 11; women recipients spurring suffragists, 21

Noise, 103–4, 106

Nonverbal communication, 34, 65; and assertive impact, 65

Nooyi, Indra, 43–45. *See also* Intuitive orientation: exemplars

Obama, Barack: androgynous leadership, 52; healthy contrition in a leader, 5–6; mother-to-son heritage, 99–102; reelection indicative of new America, 133

Obama, Michelle, 93–95. *See also* Empowering intent: exemplars

O'Keefe, Georgia, 23

Open awareness, 31, 33

Open understanding, 63, 113–14. *See also* Directive force: tool kit

Other-awareness, 30, 34. *See also* Emotional intelligence

Other-management, 30. *See also* Emotional intelligence

Overapologizing, as feminine leadership detriment, 4–7

Overcompeting, as masculine leadership detriment, 7–8

Pankhurst, Emiline, 20–21

Palin, Sarah, 60–62

Parks, Rosa, 21–22

Paul, Alice, 21

Pearl Harbor, 31, 33

Pelosi, Nancy, 134

Phenomenology, 39–40

Piaget, Jean, 50

Planning, as development tool, 63, 113. *See also* Directive force: tool kit

Political savvy: impact with integrity, 58; overly political, 58; underpolitical, 58

Power: abuses of, 58–60; empowerment and, 81; shared power as feminine leadership hallmark, 87–90, 114, 124; six bases of, 87–89, 92, 94, 114

Princess Diana, 23

Queen Elizabeth I, 17–18

Queen Elizabeth II, 17–18

Queen Victoria, 17–18

Quieting the mind, as development tool, 38–40, 113. *See also* Intuition: intuition building

Quindlen, Anna, 137

Raven, Bertram, 87. *See also* Power: six bases of

Reflection, as development tool, 38–40, 113. *See also* Intuition: intution building

Resistance, as culturally imbedded, 8, 135

Right brain: intuition and, 28–30, 38, 45, 49, 62; and intuition-building through quieting the mind and reflection, 28, 39–40; as synergistic, 64. *See also* Alter-brain behavior

Roddick, Anita, 42. *See also* Intuitive orientation: exemplars

Roosevelt, Eleanor, 10–11, 14, 68–69. *See also* Directive force: exemplars

Sabanci, Güller, 108–9, 112. *See also* Assimilative nature: exemplars

Sanger, Margaret, 11, 14

Seldman, Marty, 32, 58

Self-awareness, 30–31, 34. *See also* Emotional intelligence

Self-management, 30. *See also* Emotional intelligence

Shared knowledge, 74–76, 90. *See also* Empowering intent

Shared mastery, 74–76. *See also* Empowering intent

Shared power, 87–90, 114, 124. *See also* Empowering intent

Shinn, Florence Scovel, 27

Stanton, Elizabeth Cady, 21

Steinem, Gloria, 23, 137

Stewart Martha, 65–66. *See also* Directive force: exemplars

Storytelling, 90. *See also* Empowering intent: how to empower

Stowe, Harriet Beecher, 138

Sweeney, Patrick, and leadership qualities that distinguish women, 37

Tarule, Jill Mattuck, and feminist perspective on learning, 75. *See also* Shared knowledge; Shared mastery; Shared power

Team development, as a function of leadership, 82, 90–92, 115

Tett, Gillian, interview with Christine Lagarde, 41. *See also* Lagarde, Christine

Thatcher, Margaret, 18, 47, 56–58

Troianello, Christine, 121–24, 135

Truth, Sojourner, 21–22

Tubman, Harriet, 10, 14, 21

Walker, Madame C. J., 42. *See also* Intuitive orientation: exemplars

West, Mae, 138

Winfrey, Oprah, 42, 65–67. *See also* Directive force: exemplars; Intuitive orientation: exemplars

Winnicott, Donald, 83–84, 86

Women-owned businesses, 43. *See also* Intuitive orientation: exemplars

Women's intuition, 27–28, 36, 45. *See also* Intuition; Intuitive; Intuitive orientation

Yi, Wu, 55–56

Yousufzai, Malala, 117, 132, 135

Zenger, Jack, and leadership effectiveness, 24–25

About the Foreword Author

Carla L. Picardi has a degree in architecture and design and over 30 years' experience in leading people to create a vision and to make that vision a reality in design, property development, concept development, project management, and people development. Carla was awarded the prestigious Loeb Fellowship for Advanced Environmental Studies at Harvard University Graduate School of Design for her work on Canary Wharf in London, where she was one of the original eight people who created the concept and one of the project executives who implemented Phase 1. Carla was the project director for the preconstruction phase of the iconic Gherkin in London, which received the first planning permission in over 30 years for a tall building in the City of London and won the 2004 Stirling Prize for architecture.

Carla has been a vice president for Citibank and a strategic development adviser to the BBC. She consults on architectural projects of all sizes and lectures on design, complex development projects, leadership, coaching, and various other topics. Carla is a certified professional coactive coach and a member of the International Coach Federation; she coaches students and executives worldwide. She lives in Asolo, Italy, with her husband, Goffredo Chiavelli.

ABOUT THE AUTHOR AND THE LEAD LIFE INSTITUTE

Mary Lou Décosterd, PhD, is founder and managing executive of the Lead Life Institute, a leadership-psychology consultancy offering programs and services to help executives, teams, and organizations become their best. Dr. Décosterd has 25 years of experience in organizational development, applied psychology, and university teaching and is the author of three leadership books, including: *Right Brain/Left Brain Leadership: Shifting Style for Maximum Impact* and *Right Brain/Left Brain President: Barack Obama's Uncommon Leadership Ability and How We Can Each Develop It.* Dr. Décosterd has also written and published a children's book entitled *Magical Max Makes Friends, a* philanthropic work aimed at supporting the character development of young readers and getting books to children in need.

Dr. Décosterd is adept at assessing individual and organizational needs and obtaining results. She works as a seasoned executive coach to leaders and leadership teams and as a facilitator, speaker, trainer, and training designer for organizations. Her areas of expertise include leadership development, implementation and execution, cultural and team development and alignment, wellness, and work/life integration.

Dr. Décosterd has lived and worked in the United States and abroad. She is a graduate of the University of Hartford, the University of Oklahoma, and the Fielding Institute. She holds a BA in psychology; master's degrees in educational psychology, organizational development, and clinical psychology;

postmaster's certification in community/school psychology; and a PhD in human development. She has been recognized by "Who's Who in Teaching" and "Outstanding Women of America."

The Lead Life Institute is a leadership consultancy offering dynamic programs and services to help executives and their teams realize their potential and become their best. Recognizing the challenges, opportunities, and complexities of today's world, the Lead Life Institute provides state-of-the-art approaches for business and organizational success. As our name indicates, we focus on the successful integration of leadership and life skills. For us, *leadership* is a broad term encompassing business and professional acumen, how we favorably impact the world, and how we make a difference. The "life" piece focuses on attitude, interpersonal power, and resilience. Our overall aim is to help individuals and organizations attain next-level success through sound strategic leadership and strong, aligned operating cultures. More specifically, the Lead Life Institute offers executive coaching and leadership development, women's leadership seminars, team excellence work, and training design and delivery.

ABOUT THE SERIES EDITOR AND ADVISORY BOARD

SERIES EDITOR

Chris E. Stout, PsyD, MBA, is a licensed clinical psychologist and a clinical full professor at the University of Illinois College of Medicine's Department of Psychiatry. He served as a nongovernmental-agency special representative to the United Nations. He was appointed to the World Economic Forum's Global Leaders of Tomorrow, and he has served as invited faculty at its annual meeting in Davos. He is the founding director of the Center for Global Initiatives. Stout is a fellow of the American Psychological Association, past president of the Illinois Psychological Association, and a distinguished practitioner in the National Academies of Practice. Stout has published or presented over 300 papers and 30 books and manuals on various topics in psychology. His works have been translated into six languages. He has lectured across the nation and internationally in 19 countries, visiting six continents and almost 70 countries. He was noted as being "one of the most frequently cited psychologists in the scientific literature" in a study by Hartwick College. He is the recipient of the American Psychological Association's International Humanitarian Award.

ADVISORY BOARD

Bruce Bonecutter, PhD, is director of behavioral services at the Elgin Community Mental Health Center, the Illinois Department of Human Services state hospital serving adults in greater Chicago. He is also a clinical assistant professor of psychology at the University of Illinois at Chicago (UIC). A clinical psychologist specializing in health, consulting, and forensic psychology, Bonecutter is also a longtime member of the American Psychological Association Taskforce on Children and the Family. He is a member of organizations including the Association for the Treatment of Sexual Abusers, the Alliance for the Mentally Ill, and the Mental Health Association of Illinois.

Joseph Flaherty, MD, is chief of psychiatry at the University of Illinois Hospital, a professor of psychiatry at the University of Illinois College of Medicine, and a professor of community health science at the UIC College of Public Health. He is a founding member of the Society for the Study of Culture and Psychiatry. Dr. Flaherty has been a consultant to the World Health Organization, to the National Institutes of Mental Health, and also the Falk Institute in Jerusalem. He has been director of undergraduate education and graduate education in the Department of Psychiatry at the University of Illinois. Dr. Flaherty has also been staff psychiatrist and chief of psychiatry at Veterans Administration West Side Hospital in Chicago.

Michael Horowitz, PhD, is president and professor of clinical psychology at the Chicago School of Professional Psychology, one of the nation's leading not-for-profit graduate schools of psychology. Earlier, he served as dean and professor of the Arizona School of Professional Psychology. A clinical psychologist practicing independently since 1987, his work has focused on psychoanalysis, intensive individual therapy, and couples therapy. He has provided disaster mental health services to the American Red Cross. Horowitz's special interests include the study of fatherhood.

Sheldon I. Miller, MD, is a professor of psychiatry at Northwestern University and director of the Stone Institute of Psychiatry at Northwestern Memorial Hospital. He is also director of the American Board of Psychiatry and Neurology, director of the American Board of Emergency Medicine, and director of the Accreditation Council for Graduate Medical Education. Dr. Miller is also an examiner for the American Board of Psychiatry and Neurology. He is founding editor of the *American Journal of Addictions* and founding chairman of the American Psychiatric Association's Committee on

Alcoholism. Dr. Miller has also been a lieutenant commander in the U.S. Public Health Service, serving as psychiatric consultant to the Navajo Area Indian Health Service at Window Rock, Arizona. He is a member and past president of the Executive Committee for the American Academy of Psychiatrists in Alcoholism and Addictions.

Dennis P. Morrison, PhD, is chief executive officer at the Center for Behavioral Health in Indiana, the first behavioral health company ever to win the JCAHO Codman Award for excellence in the use of outcomes management to achieve health care quality improvement. He is president of the Board of Directors for the Community Healthcare Foundation in Bloomington and has been a member of the Board of Directors for the American College of Sports Psychology. He has served as a consultant to agencies including the Ohio Department of Mental Health, the Tennessee Association of Mental Health Organizations, the Oklahoma Psychological Association, the North Carolina Council of Community Mental Health Centers, and the National Center for Heath Promotion in Michigan. Morrison served across 10 years as a Medical Service Corps officer in the U.S. Navy.

William H. Reid, MD, is a clinical and forensic psychiatrist and a consultant to attorneys and courts throughout the United States. He is clinical professor of psychiatry at the University of Texas Health Science Center. Dr. Reid is also an adjunct professor of Psychiatry at Texas A&M College of Medicine and Texas Tech University School of Medicine, as well as a clinical faculty member at the Austin Psychiatry Residency Program. He is chairman of the Scientific Advisory Board and Medical Advisor to the Texas Depressive & Manic-Depressive Association, as well as an examiner for the American Board of Psychiatry & Neurology. He has served as president of the American Academy of Psychiatry and the Law, as chairman of the Research Section for an International Conference on the Psychiatric Aspects of Terrorism, and as medical director for the Texas Department of Mental Health and Mental Retardation. Dr. Reid earned an Exemplary Psychiatrist Award from the National Alliance for the Mentally Ill. He has been cited on the Best Doctors in America listing since 1998.

About the Series

THE PRAEGER SERIES IN CONTEMPORARY PSYCHOLOGY

In this series, experts from various disciplines peer through the lens of psychology, telling us answers they see for questions of human behavior. Their topics may range from humanity's psychological ills—addictions, abuse, suicide, murder, and terrorism among them—to works focused on positive subjects including intelligence, creativity, athleticism, and resilience. Regardless of the topic, the goal of this series remains constant—to offer innovative ideas, provocative considerations, and useful beginnings to better understand human behavior.

Series Editor
Chris E. Stout, PsyD, MBA
Founding Director, Center for Global Initiatives
Clinical Professor, College of Medicine, University of Illinois at Chicago

Advisory Board
Bruce E. Bonecutter, PhD
University of Illinois at Chicago
Director, Behavioral Services, Elgin Community Mental Health Center

Joseph A. Flaherty, MD
University of Illinois College of Medicine and College of Public Health
Chief of Psychiatry, University of Illinois Hospital